Can I Tell You a Secret?

Live Poets @ Don Bank
Can I Tell You a Secret?

Edited by Danny Gardner

Can I Tell You a Secret?
ISBN 978 1 76041 051 3
Copyright © text individual contributors 2015
Front cover design by Danny Gardner and Shuang Wu;
illustration by Sue Bacsi
Back cover design by Danny Gardner and Shuang Wu;
image of Don Bank cottage courtesy of North Sydney Council

First published 2015 by
GINNINDERRA PRESS
PO Box 3461 Port Adelaide 5015 Australia
www.ginninderrapress.com.au

Contents

Preface		11
4 April 1990		14
Introduction		16
2005		**20**
Of Poetry	Peter Boyle	28
The Poem That Escaped	Bogdan Koca	29
Sometimes the man & his wife go away	Elisabeth Hodgson	33
The Up Train	Dennis McDermott	34
My Shoebox ID	Willem Tibben	35
Tunnel of Ants	Brian Purcell	36
September Song	David Tribe	38
Mist and Mellow Fruitfulness	Sue Hicks	40
2006		**43**
Mingmarriya Country	Margaret Bradstock	52
Penelope on the Beach	Phil Radmall	54
So You Took a Trip	Robert Balas	56
Red Sails	Charles Lovecraft	58
At the Olympics: Handball	Martin Langford	59
From a train in Connecticut	David Musgrave	60
Death by Dissonance	Jennifer Maiden	62
boxing day test	Cecilia White	63
Meeting the Relatives	Richard Tipping	64
The Fridge is Pregnant	Dan Eggs	65
Pārvatī in Darlinghurst	Michelle Cahill	66
Forgotten Nectar in the Sleeper's Cave	Richard James Allen	67
Poetry and Presenting it in Public	**Part One**	**68**
2007		**77**
Listening for the road	Louise Oxley	86
salon	joanne burns	87
White, Whitely, Whitest	Louise Wakeling	88
November Evening–Nottingham Castle	Thomas Thorpe	89

Polling Day	Bob Howe	90
Stranded Noah's Ark	Ketut Yuliarsa	91
By the river	Isil Cosar	92
Public Tree	Fadeel Kayat	93
Mama Named Her Paris France	Paul Buckberry	94
The Sea Dragon's Tale	Bee Perusco	96
Hauntings	Carolyn Gerrish	98
2008		**100**
Scatter Pattern	Stephen Edgar	111
Shells	Brendan Doyle	112
Cross-examination…	Peter Wagner	113
Sunday Sailor	Henry Sheerwater	115
Happy Endings	Craig Powell	117
Atget's Paris 1898–1927	Pip Griffin	118
The New Cooking	Ross Hattaway	119
Vicky Viidikas in 1974	Mario Licón-Cabrera	120
My Sister	John Tranter	121
Ubuntu e chalo…	Dorothy Makasa	122
Truculence (Teen Valkyrie)	Cathy Bray	123
Flickatharist	Stephen Jurd	124
Poetry and Presenting it in Public	**Part Two**	**125**
2009		**132**
The Right Fundamentals	Jenny Campbell	140
Terror Australis	Leigh Blackmore	144
A Deathless Love	Margaret Curtis	146
Dumpling	Cherie	148
A Tamil Mother's Laugh!	Bhagavadas Sriskanthadas	149
Letter from Oz	Dona Samson Zappone	150
Marriage	Emily Ballou	151
Small Beginnings	Maurice Whelan	153
Greenwich Village (1980)	Barvara Hush	154
Pointy Toes	Carol Nelson	155
2010		**157**

Transported	Sheryl Persson	165
My Darling, It's Late	Mark Tredinnick	166
In the time of war	Tatiana Bonch-Osmolovskaya	167
Call Waiting	Ava Banerjee	168
Mothers	Carolyn Lowry.	170
Their eyes disturb us	Phyllis Perlstone	171
Hindered by the Hearth	Les Wicks	172
NYC – poetry bars	Steve Smart	173
sorry	Randall Stephens	174
The Donation	Susan Adams	175
Seeds of Change	George Clark	177
By Ourselves, Nothing?	Roberta Lowing	178
Dis Place	Nur J Alam	180
In Between Fairytales	Brian Bell	181
Poetry and Presenting it in Public	**Part Three**	**183**
2011		**190**
Found Poem, Cooma	Tug Dumbly	199
Sacrifice	Mary Tang	202
The Fear	Omar Musa	203
A Revolution: Televised	Rich Blk	205
The Dig Tree	Anna Kerdijk Nicholson	207
the moon on her setting arc	Jackson	211
A Spade By Any Other Name	Clark Gormley	213
Tiger	Paul Giles	214
I Have Poems	Billy Marshall Stoneking	215
Round flat tin	Christina Conrads	216
Brothers	David L Falcon	217
Man and Moisturiser	Ross Donlon	218
Australian Language Landscape	Ludwika Amber	219
Ode to Coffee	Carol Jenkins	220
Garlic	Christopher Wallace-Crabbe	221
2012		**223**
My Poems in Russian	Nora Krouk	232

The Ordinary Order of Things	David Wansbrough	233
Sea Heaver	Mike Richter	236
Stealing Paradise	Lou Steer	237
Borderlines	Jenni Nixon	239
A Little Laugh I Lost Somewhere	Skye Loneragan	241
Heartland	Ed Wilson	243
On Shanghai Road	Anthony Scanlon	244
She Chucked a Sickie	Benito Di Fonzo	245
Dear God	Ten Ch'in Ü	247
Poetry and Presenting it in Public	**Part Four**	**250**
2013		**257**
Carapace	Dexter Dunphy	267
Almanac	Kate Lilley	269
Carnaby's Cockatoo	Robert Adamson	270
On the Waterfront In Genoa…	Jennifer Compton	272
Seraphim's Dance	Carole Abourjeili	273
Waiting	Catherina Behan	274
Eveleigh Street	Keith Hansen	276
An *anniversaire* of insomnia	Ariel Riveros Pavez	279
On a far journey	Ouyang Yu	281
Woman	Nancy Louka	283
Wordless	Scott Sandwich	287
For Séraphine	Tineke Van der Eecken	289
Sister green tree frog	Ray Wittenberg	292
2014		**295**
Sonnet	Brenda Saunders	306
Coleface	Verdon Morcombe	307
Dodgy Dick the Fracking Engineer	Des Pensable	308
43	Jacqueline Buswell	309
Herbal Tea	Kyla Lee Ward	311
Haiku Walk	Helen Wren	313
Wild Wind	Assad Cina	314
Dancing Sinatra	David Reiter	315

Footlock	Marie McMillan	317
Storm	Kerry Jamieson	319
Nursing Distraction	Kristin Hannaford	321
Are We There Yet?	Ember Flame	322
The Connoisseur	Erwin Zehentner	325
Our Distracted Hands	Susan Sleepwriter	326
I am Jamal Al-Hallaq	Jamal al Hallaq	327
Home Away From Home	Yarrie Bangura	328
Poetry and Presenting it in Public	**Part Five**	**329**
2015		**337**
A Peaceful Time	Bhupen Thakker	340
Glass Mirror	Olga Kulanowska	341
Scenes from a 24-hour News Channel	Ben Hession	342
River Music	Judith Beveridge	343
The Clock	La Shawna Talisha	344
Night Graffiti	Jill Carter-Hansen.	345
Reunion of the Source	Hamish Danks Brown	346
Bathurst Street	Fayroze Lutta	348
To the whales at Warrnambool	Beth Spencer	351
My Teacher Fish	Jim Quealey	352
Stormy Ocean	Amory Hill	353
Circle	Eileen Chong	354
Basra	Ahmad Al Rady	355
Towards Melaleuca	Danny Gardner	356
Afterword – 22 April 2015		**357**
Acknowledgements		**360**
Thanks		**362**

This book is dedicated to Martin Harrison
and Nashaa Abdul-Hassan

'farewell is not goodbye'

Preface

Shakespeare has said it already: 'There is nothing new under the sun.'

There is nothing inherently new about what poets say to their audience. It is more how they say it and that they are ready to say it to strangers. Ready to exist at that moment via their beliefs; to live their thoughts and feelings. To let us into their secrets.

There is an arcane intimacy in that process, that exchange between the poet and his listener. That can't be replicated by any other art form or computer-aided simulation.

Welcome to Live Poets @ Don Bank (née Live Poets' Society) at 25.

Concentrating on the years 2005 to 2015, this book is as much about the venue and how it operates as it is about the poems or the poets.

We hope you enjoy the secrets within…

'Just our eyes were hearing and speaking' – anonymous

'the space between what is and what might be'
– Sonya Hartnett

'No person can be explained by their personal history, least of all a poet' – Katherine Anne Porter

'The world is never the same once a good poem has been added to it' – Dylan Thomas

'Poetry is the only art people have not yet learned to consume – like soup' – anonymous

4 April 1990

It is raining cats and dogs just as soon we hope it will be raining metaphors and similes. It is the first night of our new venture. It's called the Live Poets' Society. We have a small, cleared space in a Neutral Bay café. I have just carried an ironing board through the streets from our flat in Cremorne covered with a plastic garbage bag. Not only poets are coming – we are also featuring a local musician and he will balance his keyboard on the ironing board to weave his magic. It is all part of the logistics for the unpaid courier (myself). Along with the change tin, the sign-in book, the book or two we will read from – the ambition to get something going. The café cook is busy preparing the pasta and various sauces and salads that patrons will enjoy along with the poetry and music for the set entry price. All the tables and chairs are waiting to receive them and the time for the opening bell is approaching. Sue Hicks, the co-founder and MC, comes up to go through a final checklist with me. She and her friends, Cathy Stace and Les Currie, were the masterminds behind this crazy idea.

'Why should people have to go to the city or to Balmain to enjoy good poetry live?' was the cry that night in the pub. There must be lots of poets and unplugged musos on the North Shore. They can't all be Wynyard and Bridge Street business office workers, can they?

Cathy said we could run the event at the café she manages, L'Orangerie in Neutral Bay, one block back from Military Road. 'We need something to get people in on Wednesday nights.'

What would we call the event?

'You could name it after that movie that had Robin Williams in it,' Les Currie, theatre producer and, okay, movie buff, said with a grin: 'The Dead Poets Society. But you could be the Live Poets Society!'

Sue had plenty of contacts from her job as a journo on the *Mosman Daily* and publicity would be no problem. So the plan was set that night in the Oaks. And a couple of days later, it still seemed like a goer.

And tonight, 4 April, we've secured the appearance of poetry doyenne Vera Newsom as our inaugural guest. She should be here shortly – once she makes it through this pouring rain. She's getting a lift from Balmain with a friend. Thankfully the supermarket parking area is only a block away.

We look out from the café entrance again. The rain does seem to be easing – and aren't those people looking this way? Poets are nothing if not optimistic!

Let's keep poetry live!

Danny Gardner, Sydney, 4 April 2015

Introduction

Twenty-five years ago today, Live Poets was born, was passed around, received with appropriate oohs and aahs (OK, I'm stretching it a bit) and, like most new life, grew and grew and grew. I am absolutely thrilled that Danny Gardner has kept the word and music venture going throughout the twelve years since I left Sydney to reach this silver anniversary, a real milestone.

I know what hard work it was on top of two very full-time jobs plus freelance work when we ran it together, love it though we did. As well as booking guests, liaising with the council over insurance and other matters, buying food and drink for the interval, doing publicity, making posters, reassuring people who had never read or performed in public before, answering oddball queries about everything from whether tomatoes on offer contained pips to was there a ghost at Don Bank (to the latter, no! But there is a very hungry possum who has raided the food tables in the courtyard!), there were the practical matters of arranging the chairs, running the raffle, selling the books, paying the guests, organising the open section (so many people only wanted to be on in the first half!) putting out the food, opening the wine and juice offerings and emceeing on the night as well as sitting at the door taking names and money – a major undertaking for one person, but one we had worked out well as a team of two.

Bill Tibben, a poet of some note, was the main person to step in and help Danny after I left and I know others have worked hard for the cause when and where they could. To them all, a massive thank you; your good-humoured help has kept Live Poets very alive and definitely kicking!

Between us, Danny and I edited or co-edited eight books after I set up Live Poets' Press, partly to honour the quality of much of the work from the poets who came to our events, partly to offer another publishing opportunity as many Australian publishers either closed or contracted their poetry lists. We weren't very good at the business stuff, subsidising it quite heavily and always working for free and sometimes living with piles of unsold books!

Sometimes we were overwhelmed by the generosity of some local individuals and businesses, quietly helping with the finance for launches or publication with instructions not to publicise their help. Others helped by serving drinks, designing book covers, proofreading, laying out books, offering computer skills, giving halls rent free, singing in choirs to mark the events. Such support was always given in great good spirit – and was overwhelming for us.

So I am delighted that Danny has edited this the ninth Live Poets volume in the silver anniversary year. It reflects the many vibrant changes he has made over the past thirteen years: the guest interviews, the theme nights, the genial competitions, as well as the continued vibrant writing and reading. Arts organisations never stand still and this one has grown hugely in stature thanks to Danny's determination to keep it on the Sydney arts scene and the ever-growing support base from singers, storytellers, poets and musicians.

Live Poets has always attracted visiting poets from overseas, people reading in their first language and then translation, shy newcomers and performance experts, making it a fascinating mix.

Poets of national and international note, including Les Murray, Robert Gray, Robert Adamson, Jennifer Maiden, Judith Beveridge, to name just a few, have read at Live Poets, as well as folks taking their first tentative steps and poets heard at many readings – and our philosophy has always been that everyone is welcome, everyone is valued. That has never changed and one of the thrills for us was never knowing who would walk through the door and what gem they might share.

Congratulations to everyone concerned – especially Danny – and I hope this book sells out in a flash! And that there is celebration throughout the poetry world. I'll raise a glass in England. It is a remarkable achievement and a joyous, creative one. Happy 25th Birthday Live Poets@Don Bank. Will you still be here in another quarter of a century? Watch this space!

Sue Hicks, Live Poets' co-founder, Preston, England
April 2015

social

What Live Poets' Society 15-year anniversary
Where Don Bank Museum, North Shore
When Wednesday, April 27
Who North Shore poets

Guests at the Live Poets' Society partied in style last week as readers past and present gathered to celebrate its 15-year anniversary. Famous poet Walt Whitman once said: "To have great poets there must be great audiences too," and there was certainly a first-rate crowd who came to hear readings interspersed by snippets of society history.
The crowd converged in the courtyard, where a medieval party followed. Patrons listened to acoustic band Wayward, who entertained with their unique set of instruments including the hurdy-gurdy, harp, pipes and a single drum.
An a cappella karaoke competition came next, with all entries singing impressively without word sheets. The performances were followed by a Riddle Barrel contest, which involved plenty of Poet's Corner wine being drunk and won.

Waxing lyrical

Just a quick word . . . from a society of seriously poetic aficionados that is.
Report Caroline Botting. Photos Katrina Percival.

2005

For Live Poets at Don Bank admin, it's known as the February curse. While you remember the best parts of how the previous year ended up (in November) you're never quite sure what will happen when you open the doors again. Weird things tend to happen in February.

This year, our first special guests were Kerry Leves and Phillip Hammial. The evening was billed as the Blue Mountains Men come to Don Bank. Phil read from *In the Lord of Our Slaughtered Children* but he also has another persona as a practitioner of Outsider Art. Phil's tenses and emphases tend to be clearer when read out in the right way – but he rarely engenders warmth or intimacy. A bevy of verbal acrobatics generally obtained – three-legged races with the skeleton of his mother, ten storylets of suicide, surrealist word-game endings, the gestural and the automatic colliding in the flourishes of rogue pierrots, the voice of the village shaman who no one rises to challenge – all met with chuckles of half-wonderment as applause confirmed endings.

Kerry Leves on the other hand expanded from the banal to the perfume of a rich and generous India in 'A Shrine to Lata Mengashkar'. But the journey started in London. Kerry developed his characters but his respective 'I's were never meant to be static. He finished with the soul's birds flying into the eternal.

In the open section, Dulcie Meadows remembered a Live Poets character, the late Ian Thomas. Amory Hill was left in the garden looking over where he had buried his beloved – a play-act that the audience only 'got' at the last moment.

Dennis Enright wrapped his impressions of the night's offerings in a ditty about them – as was his wont. His comment about a Kerry Leves piece, however, meant the February curse had arrived. 'Sorry to be sounding like Maria Callas, but that was too f— insulting!' Kerry said. 'You don't look happy,' Dennis offered a trifle owlishly. 'What is this – the Gong Hour?' Kerry returned. 'When does it toll for you?' Dennis's candle sputtered to a stop soon after.

March was the last chance for people to get an eligible poem in the anthology *Light on Don Bank*. Live Poets would celebrate fifteen years' life in April.

The aforementioned Dennis Enright had a guest spot along with Tricia Dearborn reading from *Frankenstein's Bathtub*. Tricia was polished and professional. Her poetry snuck up on you – but had the audience got all the nuances? Her 'Tongues' with its subtle intrigue was a highlight.

Dennis had been working up poems on the spot before the evening got started. He used rhyme as a crux rather than risk invention over some pretty hot subjects – like John Howard and 9/11 and so on. There were also some evocative pieces from his past in Zimbabwe. He had a book planned (some wag suggested to me it would other people's poetry followed by his comments).

Jenny Campbell's 'Falluja' in the second half was simply stunning. Her delivery and commitment were compulsive.

The occasion of our fifteenth birthday drew the attention of the local press with a nice two-page spread. There was a massive open section either side of a Shakespearean banquet. Music was provided by the Wayward group of Elizabethan-costumed players in the courtyard with its lute, hurdy-gurdy and death-drum (circa 1600s Tyborn). An a cappella contest was won by the show of hands for Jennifer Lee's rendition of 'Amazing Grace'. People won prizes for answering questions they pulled from a riddle barrel (another heritage from Olde Englande town fairs). Moira Bench was the highlight of the open section (got rolling by Live Poets originals Joan Aronsten and Maureen Maguire) with her theatrical rendering of a cheating lover's comeuppance. Maureen's son Nick was the youngest reader and showed a glimpse of future promise. Mark Gavier was on hand to film the proceedings for posterity.

May saw the visit of formidable playwright Bogdan Koca to Don Bank. Some of the titles of Bogdan's productions may set the scene: 'The Last Sentence Before Execution' (with obvious echoes of Guantanamo) – 'The Poem that Escaped' and 'The Poem that Exploded'. And who could forget his telephone call to God at the Gleebooks launch of the anthology *Mood Lightning* last year? Bogdan wants to usurp all our preconceptions in his seminal vision of what writing is, where expression should go, saying, 'If we are living we are challenged,' and taking us into the viscera of that experience. He has another famous saying: 'A poem becomes a poem only after it has been read by another person.' I asked him, 'Even if it's only read by the cleaner after a performance?' He laughed. 'Sometimes at my plays the cleaning doesn't take very long!'

In contrast to Bogdan's experience, Penelope Evans was debuting her first book of poems, *Cross Hatched* – in which she takes a walk from Centennial Park to the Bourbon and Beefsteak, Kings Cross – meeting characters on life's way. The small crowd lapped up her immediacy and honesty of expression.

In the open section, David Tribe reiterated an hilarious overhearing of mobile phone ranters in public spaces. And Benito di Fonzo arrived with some friends to relate a piece about a road trip towards remote Hay (NSW) with a gang of city poets – among them Tug Dumbly and A.J. Rochester mit spouse and baby. Why towards Hay? That's where the car finally ran out of fuel.

The June guests were Peter Boyle and Joanne Featherstone. Peter read mostly from his accomplished collection *Museum of Space*, which indulged the dreamlike in a jottings style: a thinking, meditative poetry rather than calculated. He also read his translations of Venezuelan and Spanish poets.

Joanne Featherstone, as director of Sydney's Red Room Poetry Project, derives energy from the different poets' voices she's worked with. These tended to get attention before her own poetry problems – as is the common fate of convenors. Her own writing has an engaging, uncomplicated colloquial facility. Joanne is an adroit interpreter of other poets' works and this night vividly evinced the works of David Prater, Ian McBryde, Jane Gibian and Fiona Wright. A Luke Davies piece from *Totem*, what's more, simply took on wings before our eyes.

July saw a night of Indigenous poetry from Dennis McDermott and Elisabeth Hodgson, and readings from *Ngara*, an anthology edited by Martin Langford and John Muk Muk Burke, where Indigenous and non-Indigenous writers discussed 'living in this place now'.

McDermott, cosy with his listeners, was passionate but understated by turns – rhythm and unity underwrote his approach and he communicated his erudition with authority leavened with humorous touches. A simple train ride to the Blue Mountains, for instance, became an elegy in his hands. A haunting from his past often demanded attention nevertheless.

But not to the extent of Wiradjuri woman Elisabeth Hodgson from Wollongong, who arrived, jokingly as she said, with her bodyguard – a sister to get her to and from the train on time. Elisabeth was charming but unerring – taking us back to her stolen childhood in evocations, from her schoolyard pals to home where she lived among her adopted tribe. This pattern of going from hand to hand to seek yet risk reliance, to fit in, continued as an adult, from husband number one to number two and sole parenting, a process that marks her work with an honesty that's impressed the likes of Judith Beveridge, no less.

As surely as the nail in the wall where a painting has been taken down in her white house, fixed the flickering, home-movie images of Aboriginals that have found solace in Christianity. Elisabeth states boldly, 'My life cannot be painted onto a canvas – it is a skin painting.' Elisabeth would be on her way next month to a poetry festival she'd been invited to in Struga, Macedonia. The book *Ngara* is impressive and no less poignant in its purpose and celebration than a stockman's unanswered question to tribesmen undergoing the first pangs of colonialism, 'So where is your country?'

August's focus was a tribute to the work of former English Poet Laureate Ted Hughes – in all its phases from 'Hawk Roosting' through 'Crow' and 'the River' and poems for Sylvia (Plath). So surprised was he at how powerful Hughes' work, as presented, was local performance poet Cliff Flax immediately wanted to know where he could buy copies of all his books.

A person in the open section who presented as Phil/Sandra was ready to go to New York to compete in that city's marathon as him/herself.

There was an open section theme: Poets' Poets. Who has Influenced You Most? which proved instructive. Bill Tibben read ee cummings and Hughes' 'Thought Fox'. Les Wicks read a NZ poet who died young. Ted, partner of Pip Griffin and from NZ, read a poem from Atilla the Stockbroker – an out-there operator from this convenor's London years. Maureen Ten read a Shakespeare sonnet and John Carey offered up bons mots from Wallace Stevens.

Martin Harrison arrived in September to guest along with Kathielyn Job from Dubbo. Martin did a lovely version of 'Thinking of Rain' and an aching prose piece from the book *Summer*, which included the elegiac 'A Dog Barking'. He talked of his work on the Creating Australia project and reflected on how our country affects the writer's psyche – even European writers, even a recently arrived Yorkshireman like himself.

Kathielyn's poetry was evocative with homely refrains – melaleuca legends with reference to her recent book. But there was one piece that paraphrased Donald Rumsfeld's sayings and another published by Les Murray in *Quadrant* that fell one word at a time down the page, obtuse – experimental enough to make the Black Inc *Best Poems of 2004*.

In the open section, Barbara Fisher hinted how the hurt and the harrowing can lurk in the seemingly envious. Cliff Flax this time round seemed to be trying too hard to be disturbing while John Carey came across as malefic and predatory. Sue Wildman – first time back after a while – stuffed the last line of a misremembered 'Beyond Blue' but the jewels in that piece still shone.

October's edition: Our Thoughts are Our Business featured a non-poet – Jenny Zeng recently emigrated from China – and longtime Live Poets stalwart Bill Tibben, whose book *The Fascination of What's Simple* had recently been launched.

Jenny Zeng's story of being persecuted by the Chinese government for her following of the Falun Gong spiritual group is searing. Her family has been carved in two by it. Born in 1966 in Sichuan province, Jenny graduated from Beijing University in 1991. She began studying Falun Gong in 1997. Two years later, she was arrested and sent to a work camp for a year to be rehabilitated in the Communist faith. In 2001 Jenny sought asylum in Australia with her daughter. In 2004 she was given refugee status. Her husband, who was urged by the authorities to get Jenny to renounce Falun Gong – and who has been falsely accused of being in the group himself – is still in China. Jenny worries for his safety as he has been imprisoned for brief periods for disobedience. All the freedoms we have as poetry groups, as individuals, to express ourselves free of government censure, we take for granted. We all know Communist China is not a democracy. We all know a country has to be governed. We can appreciate some of the difficulties and pressures of a vastly changing society such as China is. But when the government – any government – interferes with our spiritual lives, our conversation with our souls, that is where a line must be drawn.

Jenny's book *Witnessing History* is prose but the implications it contains can be related to by any writer. One of the most chilling passages Jenny read out involved her finally leaving her job to have a secret holiday with her husband and daughter – away from the suffocating pressure of the authorities and the attention of her neighbours and peers. As the family sank collectively on the bed in their hotel room in a faraway town, Jenny took a phone call. 'Welcome, Jenny, to the first day of your well-earned holiday.' It was the local chapter of the Communist party letting her know Jenny was in their purview now. 'We hope you enjoy your time here.'

The change of pace after the supper break was palpable, with Bill's poems about families, situations and country. The poem for his mother written as he went through her glory box after her death was achingly vivid. There was lots of humour and irony too. One piece called 'Showering on the Nullarbor' was in two voices – one inside and one outside a train's bathroom cubicle at speed. It later became a performance piece for Running Order – a performance troupe Bill's in with Danny Gardner and Maureen Ten.

The open section theme was entitled How are your thoughts under threat?

Colleen Burke and Brian Purcell rounded out the year as special guests for November. Colleen was reading from her recently released book, which featured a retinue of wry reflections on urban life and how people in close proximity get on with each other – or not. She is a practised performer who has lent her expertise to several books of Irish writing in Australia. Her home truths reward further study as there are echoes behind her deceptively straightforward assertions.

Brian Purcell, famous in Live Poets lore for his epic poem 'A Tunnel of Ants' about the death of (ex-Princess) Diana from the book *Ten Years Live* – cited by University Professor Elizabeth Webby no less when she launched same – is also a musician. We got a double whammy then with songs from the CD of Brian's band, Distant Locusts. These were surreal and forensic observations from an eye whose perceptions about our place in the firmament will resonate in word and melody for some time to come. A thoroughly entertaining night was compounded by the ad hoc appearance of the Sydney Choir of Women – prompted by tireless Live Poets campaigner Pip Griffin – who delighted with early season Carols in the Courtyard over supper.

Of Poetry

Great poems are often extraordinarily simple.
They carry their openness
with both hands.
If there is a metaphor lounging in a doorway
they step briskly past.
The boom of generals
and presidents with their rhetoric manuals
will go on sowing the wind.

The great poems are distrustful of speech.
Quietly,
like someone very old
who has only a few hours left of human time,
they gaze into the faces around them
one by one
they kiss love into our mouths.

Peter Boyle

The Poem That Escaped

you sit in front of me
you lie in your bed
or maybe you stand in front of the wall
with me stuck onto it
in a less than glorifying fashion
or maybe you have found me in a book
somewhere between pages
or maybe you don't see me at all
and only one of my words captures your attention
and then you stop and you glance at me

I am the poem that escaped

I had enough
I have been used for so many trivial purposes
I've been imprisoned
modified reshaped developed
so many times by an endless gallery of selfish poets
I have been used
transmitting ideas questions and answers
I have been forced to solve the problems of humanity
I have been fixing up unfulfilments
and justifying the deaths of millions
pronouncing love and hatred
denying and praising gods
I have been wearing forms and structures
tailored for me without my own permission
carrying good and bad rhymes and an uncomfortable metre

I've been dismantled and reconstructed freezing on ancient walls
and stinking between old dusty pages
supplying fame and misery hope and predictions
I've been accusing and forgiving
uniting and dividing
loving on behalf of lovers who don't know how to love
I've been crying and laughing
provoking
providing someone's solutions
for any occasion
I've been forced to communicate
all the languages of the world
without my own consent
I've been solemnly recited
for masses
on stadiums
in lavish gardens
by bards
comedians
children with red scarves over their necks
accompanied by bands
and cannons
I have been in poets' service since my verses
could safely hide their imperfections
I've been deprived of my own voice
to defraud one's lack of imagination

I am the poem that escaped

don't read me out
just look at me
don't distribute me
accept the clumsiness of my freedom
contemplate my solitude
don't tell of me
don't sing me
don't scrutinise me
just let us have an intimate hesitation
a comfortable lack of commitment
let us be silent and thoughtful
with no prejudice with no expectations
don't ever read me out
don't whisper me
using an appropriate diction
correct
clear
round
don't try to heal my wounded vowels
my crooked consonants
and don't betray me by telling poets
of me and you
you are as I am
a poem of silence
you are my kin
for
my existence

my safety
and my well-being
is in your eyes
I live without a poet
I can't exist without your sight
your permission
your will
you are in front of me
not knowing
why
what for
I won't provide you with recipes
I cannot answer any of your questions
I wish to celebrate our acquaintance in secret
outliving my eternity
at the bottom of your drawer
between things that matter
memories
old photos
and a long-forgotten collection of passion

Bogdan Koca

Sometimes the man and his wife go away

They drive to Alice Springs in their old car.
When they come back they show us slides of their trip.
On the wall there is a picture of a red rose with a biblical verse
it reads: *suffer the little children to come unto me*;
the man takes the picture down,
the wall is bare except for a big blunt nail.
When the man shows the slides I look at the nail
mostly it is in the trees or the sky.

There is a slide of an old black man. He is smiling –
his eyes are deep and dark, his teeth are white.
This is our friend Jacky says the man showing the slides.
He has another name but we just call him Jacky
and he is a Christian, says the man's wife.
The other adults in the room are pleased at this,
they murmur *Amen*; I look for the nail in the wall,
it is poking out of the black man's eye.

Another slide – a black woman, she is squinting.
This is Jacky's wife, Mary. She's a Christian too.
It was wonderful to enjoy their fellowship.

They didn't enjoy the fellowship of my parents
as they tell them their children no longer belong to them.
They held puritanical hands against their faces
to repel the alcoholic fumes,
as my father asks to see his children
for one last time.

Elisabeth Hodgson

The Up Train

There's no country: Sydney merely thins.
Desperate to get out of town, I lift streets from the soil,
digging for dirt.

To the west, half a rainbow snags clouds. The Egyptians knew
why ibis bend into the waterlogged lanes of Lidcombe Oval
like runners ignoring the gun.

Near Penrith, a hawk flaps angel wings
backwards, black mask round its head, tethered
by a sight line to the need below.

I'm heading where I can hear
crows mourn, watch wagtails swish their bums
for hours.

The train climbs Linden bush. In the valleys that fall
either side, gum blossom – fluffy as fresh pecorino – sprinkles
whole, wooded ridges. I sit back, happy

as a black cockatoo about to launch its gravity
from a bobbing pine-branch, a baby ape
with a gift pair of wings.

Dennis McDermott

My Shoebox ID

I'm sifting through a shoebox full of documents. I find a copy of the English translation of an extract from my Dutch birth registration, there are primary school reports, high school reports, my very ordinary leaving certificate results, the telegram I got from Mr Lynch, he taught me in primary school and hoped for big things from me, congratulating me anyway.

There's a lock of mum's hair – not a real one – it is hair I pulled from a comb in the days between her death and her funeral, a piece of her jewellery, paper clippings from World War Two. There is a photo of two-year-old me with Dad and he's kneeling – we're holding fish he's caught and there's a bucket.

There is a thin wad of aerograms, my naturalisation certification, a paper clipping of my first year uni results (that's better…), the copy I made of a cheque I got for a poem I wrote called 'memory bucks' that got itself published.

We live out lives of ordinary truths. Waiting for miracles we do and do not want, that we face and do not face with the mouthful of cliches we use to explain and explain away, the few phrases of regret we manage. The promises we make and break. Blink – another decade's passed.

I'm sifting through a shoebox full of documents, the things which prove who I am. This is who I am.

Willem Tibben

Tunnel of Ants

Diana, September 1997

You came with a label 'eat me' attached,
so we did, and each one
according to their needs declared

sister – lover – mother –
whore
                      bowing your head
                      accepted it all

like the woman of Samaria
drawing from an upwelling spring
the water all men crave to drink
endlessly, to see themselves in blue
ellipse of your eye, a depthless region
where they could burn
and cocking their cameras, slowly
turn to you like any lover.

                Like Jesus,
who knew all the names of your lovers.

Then you, an angel
would approach and gently
smear vaseline on their lenses –
and everything would be a blur.

It was past Kafka's midnight when you woke in a tunnel
with every leg broken, no way up, back or through,
the dung festering on your fractured shell –
just a bug, crushed in its own carapace

and almost at the last you came eyeball to eyeball
with the final intruder, the king of the ants
who carefully extended his long dark antenna

right through
                        your one
            smashed
                  and beautiful

                                          eye.

Brian Purcell

September Song

for my mother's 100th birthday

    'Congratulations, Barbara.
    A race well run,
    you've done a ton.'
The spring light glistens on the creamy
piping of the birthday cake
and on the messages propped up
before you in the nursing home.
The cards that glitter most are not
from relatives and friends (so few of them)
but from officialdom as sighing secretaries
dispense expected greetings from the great.
Lost in a fringe of flowers you sit
slumped in a wheelchair and apparent
peace, your pink cheeks hiding
jaws of death, sedated lest you
wake in fright and shriek a baby's
cry on entering an alien world.
Behind the yellow curtain of your
eyes a century unfolds: decades of wars
and epidemics and bewildering change,
the struggle to defy a plunge
into the Great Depression from whose rocks
no one escaped unscarred. Inside your head
thoughts simmer, never boiling over: romantic
dreams of journeys only made in books,
of sibling love that other families knew,
of son a doctor, not a dropout scribe,
of sweet grandchildren that were never born,

of friends who shouldn't die before yourself and
of the man who should have been your spouse.
Now all the hopes are dead inside a dying
mind, the sights and sounds outside are
fading with the failing senses.
    'Congratulations, Barbara.
    a race well run,
    you've done a ton.'

David Tribe

Mist and Mellow Fruitfulness

'Season of mist and mellow fruitfulness' –
one special letter opened with this each autumn,
throughout my university years and
for decades later, working here and in Australia,
scripted in your flowing, cursive style.
Always a walker, you celebrated the colours,
passing on your knowledge of seasons, trees,
birds and wildflowers to us as little girls
as we trekked local fields year round,
dodging cowpats, roly-polying down hills –
you joining in – looking for bluebells and birds' nests
more than half a century ago, wondering at fledglings,
new leaf and buds and autumn colours.
On rainy days you read us poems – loving Keats,
Shakespeare and Rabbie Burns – taught us how to
do handstands against the kitchen wall, skipping in the hall,
helped with scrapbooks, reading, teaching us to knit
and making sure there were laughs and stories along the way.
As the dementia kicked in, but before you forgot
how to write, several letters each autumn started the same way,
'season of mists and mellow fruitfulness',
arriving in Sydney's hot spring.
All precious. All kept. All still read.

Eleven years ago, this was your last weekend.
My father and I sat by you, talking, soothing, observing,
on guard, giving you all our love as best we could.
You drifted on morphine, in and out of sleep,
remembering your 'pleases' and 'thank yous' despite the pain.
Two whole days, two whole nights we watched over you,
willing it to be a peaceful, gentle death.
Near the end, I slipped outside, gathering
red, golden, yellow and brown leaves
strewn over the nursing home's lawn.
I spread them on your pillow – my last gift to you
before I hugged you in my arms as you slipped away,
hoping you'd see them or sense them, hear their rustle.
Now no one sends me letters starting with that famous line,
even though it is the 'season of mist and mellow fruitfulness'.

Sue Hicks

2006

Our new season had been opened a couple of weeks before at Hutley Hall, North Sydney with the release of *Light on Don Bank – Fifteen Years of Live Poets*. Both co-founders were on hand – Sue Hicks having made the trip out from the UK. This convenor was on crutches after a holiday accident while trekking at Barrington Tops National Park.

I was in better shape on 22 February when Margaret Bradstock and Stephen Oliver were the special guests. A large crowd was on hand and everything seemed set fair – except that both guests wanted to go on first! Margaret had told me a relative was expecting and she wanted to be with her after nine o'clock. Stephen Oliver said he would really appreciate going on first because he had a long drive on the morrow. He and his friends had warmed up for this eventuality with several quick drinks in the courtyard pre-reading. Margaret had asked me first and would get the nod. Stephen used chicanery in indicating he'd already got agreement with Margaret. Failing that ruse, he then suggested they could both go on first before the supper break. I didn't want empty seats after supper and demurred.

Miffed or not at being denied, Stephen and friends went back to the courtyard to drink – two poems into Margaret's guest spot. Bradstock did seem to then be rushing her delivery. A very poignant Byron Bay poem steadied her but it was not her most settled performance. She was also nervous about getting a phone call re the progress of her relative's labour. All the same, she stayed for supper and won the bottle of red wine in the raffle following.

In Stephen's reading there was a piece on the destruction of the Bamiyan Buddhas that resonated, but a lot of the others wandered into prosey travel tales. Stephen kept up a ready banter in between poems and was often playful in his delivery.

There was a stupendous open section and it was good to hear the likes of Paula McKay, Charlotte Clutterbuck and Lesley Walter again after long absences. Peter Bowden's 'Tub' from *Ten Years Live* was an early delight. Marc Marusic, in a typically bizarre ending, read a poem that recalled NSW police breaking up a meeting of philosophers that had got out of hand. Quite apt considering what had transpired earlier. But this was February after all.

March promised a variety of styles, with the diminutive Katherine Gallagher out here on holiday from the UK where she lives now, at the local launch effectively of her *After Kandinsky* book by reps of Vagabond Press. Phil Radmall meantime would give a reading of his recently completed novel, *Painting St Feoc*. I had not realised Katherine's poems were all about various Kandinsky paintings as though the Russian artist were chaperoning Katherine's journey through a life of art and literature. Phil's novel was about a man obsessed with numbers. For instance, he has arrived in a village to paint its church and uses a number system to determine how he will do the task. The village regards him as some sort of saviour but it seems he and it will nullify each other in inertia. It was not the easiest task for Phil – to read this book to an audience and have it get all the nuances.

April was billed as the Napier Street Nocturne. *The Sydney Morning Herald* played ball, even without responding to the term Nude Karaoke – this convenor's other way to say, 'A Cappella Singing Contest'. The meeting fell rather flat and the main culprit was that no musicians turned up! In fact, it was the venue's most underwhelming birthday for some time with no guests, no songs, and scarce hilarity under the starlight. It fell back on the quality of the supper! One lady, bless her, said, 'It's still really good value and you have hot food!' All the same, the cake was saved for another day.

The small crowd in May on the heels of a very busy Sydney Writers Festival was lending the year a sober edge. We had a sort of TAP Gallery comes to Live Poets repeat. A couple of years ago it had worked a treat. This time, with no popular Doctor Michael on hand with his paintings, it was a different story.

Classically trained guitarist Mary Jane Leahy backed TAP's poetry mine host Robert Balas, whose poems were featured in a recent book, *Open 24 Hours*, companioned with the work of Kings Cross and Darlinghurst-based visual artists – including a Don Bank semi-regular, Erwin Zehentner.

Robert had the serenading knack – taking you into his world with voiced thoughts in a syncopated rhythm – and Mary Jane augmented that adroitly. One of the highlights was having Catalin Anastase, a photographer also featured in *Open 24 Hours*, documenting the night. This led to some beautifully evocative portraits of the likes of David Tribe, David Morris, David Wansbrough and Peter Bowden. Mary Jane's playing got funkier and gnarlier – bringing Robert back from drifting out to sea once more – as the waltz in melody, voice and rhythm started to really cut through. Later, I began seeing a like technique being employed at other venues – not that anyone at Don Bank thought they were pioneering anything on this night; it was all being uncovered as it was happening. Perhaps Catalin was the unheard unifier at work here.

Martin Langford was booked to present his new book, *Micro Texts*, at our June meeting. Circumstances forced us to improvise and helped forge a whole new feature (of how) Live Poets presented. There was a lighting issue in the front hall where people normally entered so I had the sign-in desk inside the sitting room. I normally taped special guest readings from time to time but *Micro Texts* was more essay than poetry – a series of addresses to the things that most concern poetry.

Martin and I decided instead of a straight reading that I would interview him about the book, its content and how it came about. And the first interview of the author at Live Poets was born! They would primarily be between the special guest and myself, though the crowd could (and did) interject if they wanted to ask a question. It just seemed a better way to introduce the poet/writer, and the audience got some of the background to their work that you didn't get at most other venues. If the interview was going on too long, the restlessness of the audience proved a good indication. Sometimes, of course, things hummed along so well you could throw away the prepared questions. This night, Martin did a short reading of other poems as well, and that set the template.

In the open section, Bill Tibben read the contents of his mother's old shoebox – found after she'd gone to the retirement village – and did a duet with the convenor (accenting the two voices in 'Showering on the Nullarbor'). Michael Buhagiar read some beautiful sonnets from Christopher Brennan. Marie McMillan made her first visit to Don Bank. And Doug Nicholls shared some literary anecdotes of the reader's life in his relaxed armchair style.

July saw David Musgrave interviewed and read poems. Musgrave is a growing luminary on the scene as a publisher (principal of Puncher and Wattman) and winner of the prestigious Newcastle Prize a couple of times as a poet. He's also performed that dubious waltz with depression – otherwise known as 'walking the black dog'. We started with a laugh. David was asked, 'What made you start writing, do you think?' He replied he was 'undaunted by the millions of dollars a poet could make!'

Bill Tibben and this convenor did another duet – a tribute to Daryl Wayne Hall, who had recently passed away. Bill, who was partner with Daryl in the long running PIE – Poetry, Imagery and Expression, Parramatta – had subsequently published *Poems from the Red Notebook*, a collection of Daryl's poems and songs and memorabilia which included, hauntingly, the fragmentary nature of Daryl's last poem that he woke up to write before he lay back for the last time. It reads, 'last night…asleep…whilst sleeping…in my forest…a tree shrieked a fell.'

Doug Nicholls offered another fireside chat from a man who reads poetry every day yet never forgot Charles Bukowski's legendary dictum, 'Don't do it!'

August was the subject of another short absorbing interview (they would only get out of control much later) with the arrival of Jennifer Maiden, a poet whose work intersects with contemporary politics to a vivid extent. There are obviously dangers, not least, as she readily admits, the risk of the work dating too fast, although she countered that with the observation, 'You have to know it's going to work…in all the ways you design it – or it's soon gone [dated].'

Poets in the open section were asked to read their favourite Australian poems of all time. Marc Marusic did a Shaw Nielsen piece. Bill Tibben read Gwen Harwood and Shaw Nielsen poems. Rob Forage read Jennifer Strauss. Pip Griffin read Elizabeth Riddell. Penelope Grace read a Max Dunn piece. Penelope also delighted us with tunes on her fiddle. Les Wicks and David Musgrave came to see and hear Jennifer Maiden.

September was a very full program, with the visit of three poets from Newcastle – Richard Tipping, Cecilia White and Kylie Rose. I figured there'd be no time to do any interviews, especially with the late addition of Dan Eggs – the Blagger from Belfast. Dan was in touch only a couple of weeks before: 'I'm on a flying visit to the fair Sydney around the time of my birthday!' He asserted it was OK to squeeze him in. 'I want to go on last anyway!' What that meant was he wanted to be the very last voice heard – this would make it a very long night at the Bank.

Richard Tipping has pioneered the use of ironic text in public notices resulting in irreverent road signage like 'start of artwork' (instead of roadwork). 'No understanding at any time' (we can figure out the official equivalent); 'wrong day go back'; the T-shirt that says 'Australian Poet' which near enough borrows the logo of Australia Post.

Richard later produced Sculpture by the Sea gems and the 'Bi-Sexual Bicycle', which somewhat unfortunately can be steered from either end (they both have handlebars!). It has served as a handy tool to aspects of the City of Sydney Council's social engineering bent. Richard also designed the leaflet for Don Bank this month – the immutable Poetry at the Pub sign built around a fat schooner glass. Tipping had joined in the fun by bringing along replicas of his signs to dress the Don Bank sitting room. His fuller poems proved no less adept at irony and aural punning.

He had promised salaciously that Cecilia White would be reading erotic poems translated from the German. They did not prove to be quite that – but displayed a ready sense of humour anyway rather than 'toss it off cynical'.

Kylie Rose was the dark horse – make that edgy and black – as per her dress for the night. She'd described herself beforehand as the love-child of Sylvia Plath and Garcia Lorca and proved good to her word – clinical yet passionate by turns, technically sharp. Her portrayal of the malefic controlling child punishing her doll for a perceived misdemeanour was positively chilling.

It was all turning into a night to savour. It had started with a sung ditty from Penelope and Pip: 'And we have come because of Danny / and you know of course it's Wednesday / and yes the venue is at Don Bank / with our words to entertain you' – and so on.

And then, after all, there was Dan Eggs. It's difficult to put into words what Dan is able to do. How does he keep a straight face? He lets the audience get the joke but doesn't pre-empt. It's the way he says things rather than what he says. And it's as though he's putting it together in front of your eyes for the first time – with all the tension of failure possible – in the most hilarious fashion. People were rolling in the aisles trying not to laugh as the straight face continued to expound…

Dan was the first guest we had whose interview appeared in the local paper the week after the event. And it was on page three! He told the reporter he was aged somewhere between twenty-one and eighty-two and had been writing poetry even before he was born. He said he'd recently won an Irish Ice Cream Eating Contest – downing ten cones in record time. 'My favourite flavour is sausage!' The Blagger from Belfast. You don't earn that soubriquet lightly. Oh, and it was the best house of our year!

October. He is the only poet I know who rehearses beforehand by doing push-ups in a spare room at Don Bank. His name is Richard James Allen. He is a poet, a dancer, a yoga master, with one of the best contact bases in Sydney. He's literally filled Gleebooks upstairs with his book launches. He came to Don Bank to exercise his kamikaze mind with the audience. It was probably the most erudite interview conducted thus far, built around discussion of the human expressing itself through song, dance, movement and words in ways varying on the infinite. The veracity of which Richard is the absolute fruit. We could puzzle over how *Kamikaze Mind* was generated and/or formed itself almost despite human meddling – driven by the purity of mathematics say as much as any other discipline. Holistic vs deconstructed? Part of me doesn't want to know – just appreciate the flow you've found. It was indisputably concept first and we, the readers, completed the book's coming to life by how we chose to absorb it: read it backwards, forwards, from the middle out – it's up to you. It has a discursive unity very rare on the ground.

In the open section, Rob Forage was in rare form presenting horse racing scenes from Ovid's 'Roman Gymnasium' and Patrick Cavanagh's 'Pegasus' – the horse here is his life that's suddenly found wings. Then there was Bill Tibben's poem about the horse in Picasso's *Guernica*. Then Charles Lovecraft's poems from the *Bulletin* in the 1880s – amazing what they tell you about the period (and more horses!). Plus a poem from Mary Gilmore that you sing saying, 'I am a Fairy Man'. Where does our local poetry historian get this stuff? Penelope gave us the round of the room on her fiddle and her poem 'Present' from *Light on Don Bank*. Michael Buhagiar kept the bucolic coming with a meditation on 'Ross Farm, South Coast country' – beautifully uttered off by heart.

We closed the year with two very different voices in November. The David Unaipon Award-winning stories of Tara June Winch of Australian Aboriginal and Afghan descent – and Mark O'Flynn, poet and novelist from the Blue Mountains.

There was music to open the night from Penelope Grace and Mary Jane Leahy. Michelle Cahill found herself being a woman in New York in a tale of trapped love. Brendan Doyle offered a tribute to Dennis Kevans. Danny Lockhart evoked Edgar Allen Poe. Sherry Chan read from *Moonlight of Romance*. David Tribe shared an ironic rework of Dorothy Mackellar's 'My Country'.

Mark O'Flynn read several scenes from his novel *Grass Dogs*, making the surreal something you could find walking down the street. Though you sensed this tale of the eccentric outcast, a mentally erratic loner, might end in murder – certainly criminality of a serious sort. The invention came from enabling us to accept all the craziness and still trust the leading character's moral centre in dealing with other people. Mark's was a tactical interview – unwilling to give too much away or posit the author as greater than the work. Mark has given creative writing classes in prisons and remand centres.

I reminded Tara June Winch of some advice given to her at the Sydney Writers Festival: don't let the media swallow you up (and dilute your potential). Tara has been lauded as some kind of wunderkind of Australian literature, a young star in the UQP firmament, with her novel *Swallow the Air*, which traced her early life (but she stressed should not be taken as necessarily autobiographical). Her reading was vulnerable and frank but there was a centre holding firm behind the trauma lived and now being retold. As a single mother and mentor of several Aboriginal artists, she was already worldly beyond the original hype. Tara admitted the greatest challenge would be producing the next book – the perennial fate of the follow-up. The immediate challenge was taking care of her little one at home.

Mingmarriya Country

'my name been grow up from these hills' – Queenie McKenzie

Limestone country, flayed back
to the banded domes
        like stalled time machines
this maze of cones, crossed
into echidna dreaming.
I'm walking
        among dry creek beds
touched by combed light
beehives still glowing
in the fall of after dark.
This is 'good country', telluric,
the *djang** confirms it.

Desert saints
attuned to inner geography
could have pitched their tents here
rolled out their swags on a clear night
skirted rock holes, towering ants' nests.
Antony of Thebes
homesick for a landscape
of the imagination, the gaze
                of infinite space
a terrain becoming its own icon,
might have dreamed this desolation
                this ascetic silence.

Don't speak her name
so soon after death,
use the skin name
Nakarra.

Margaret Bradstock

* property or power said to inhabit any earth or natural feature consecrated from the Dreaming.

Penelope on the Beach

Are there no other good men out there, I ask,
enough to free the cage-rattling heart,
relieve the burdened years of memories,
or check the onslaught of life's harsh pattern;
only pale-livered warriors who will yield
like me to the slow encroachment
of the final absence of air and thought and love.
Otherwise, who finds me here helps me
with nothing of what was or what will come,
alone in this careering, unsynchronised time.
Those who wait are the first to feel
and the last to know; weaving love out of patience,
unravelling faith from faithlessness.
Even the weeds lost and stranded at my heels
obey the quiet oracle of the sea
succumbing to the tumbling waves
which, as I walk, bountifully bathe my feet
whilst erasing my soft, shallow footfalls.

Further out I see the clear sky shimmer
upon the thick meniscus of the water,
the sea's deep constancy betrayed
by the complexity of its surface,
and all my own confusions mingled there.
But before the good god calls
summoning the last tide, and the waves
retreat forever from off this shallow shore
what one great soul will yet return to me
from conquering this sea's subtle force;
and who then mock our triumph with our failings?

For far more deeply fathomed will be our cause
and far less deceiving will we be, free
from all those loose and fickle reflections
that make us only what we seem to be.

Phil Radmall

So You Took a Trip

You feel her shape
She gets the mood
What's in your mind
Leaves nothing to delude
Just a 'takeaway' thought
More now than then
It all gets lost
You begin again
To drop a word
But lose the plot
Theme seems all there
But she knows it's not
The same, somehow it is
Like in déjà vu
You remember that time?
Was that really you?… Yes, you!
She says 'No'
Thinking 'That wasn't me'
Without her knowing
That your 'he' used to be a 'she'
Without you knowing
That her 'she' has become a 'he'

So you took a trip on a dialysis drip
And she didn't know about it…
So she took a trip on a dialysis drip
And you didn't know about it…

You like her eyes
When she catches your glance
But you don't realise that
In mid-trance
She looks at you
You start to gawk
She picks up your rhyme
You're about to talk
You say 'Err… How's the weather?'
She says 'I'm into leather'
You say 'Are you now?'
She says 'Yeah, it's hot and how'
You say 'The leather?'
She says 'No. The weather'

So you took a trip on a dialysis drip
And she didn't know about it…
So she took a trip on a dialysis drip
And you didn't know about it…

Robert Balas

Red Sails

Deeply phosphorescent red sails,
        Of ruby-like hue,
Clove the nebulous night
        Upon an ocean of star dew.

Even so the emerald boat
        Made fantastic time,
Because the amber-tinted night clouds
        Brought on the dawn of rose-lime.

Then, green sands and yellow hills,
        Topaz mountains and zircon fields,
Seemed to embroider the magic mind
        In untold uncommon yields.

Like a lotus eater then,
        In the land to mind forget,
Everything else was stolen,
        But the soul was…well met.

Charles Lovecraft

At the Olympics: Handball

Overweight, and bony-jawed, she cowers,
one step at a time, up the tiers of the Dome. Someone
has got her to come here – her mother perhaps:
'They won't come again in your time!' The teams flex,
and pepper the goalies in warm-up: high-fives,
and clatter, and edge. But what draws your gaze
is the way that her whole body pleads,
in its twisted withdrawal, for the seat she can't find.
She clutches the handrail for comfort. She searches
without looking up. Such hopeful gestures:
the Def Leppard T-shirt, the limp knot of lace in her hair.
She is maybe nineteen, maybe more. But you know
when the first chance arises – some drunkard,
some brother's mad mate – she will say yes,
and pray to hold on: her bed like a plain in the dark
where there are no kind choices.
                         What horror
have we laid down here: when a girl's need
first leans like a bud towards sun – and the one thing
that happens is judgement – the great stone
that lies on our kind like the distance to God?
                         So we cannot imagine a lover:
someone whose hand turns her head in delight
and in awe at her presence here too:
smoothing aside all she's learnt of the old prohibitions –
wonder, attentiveness, bubbling, upwelling –
like the pooling of permission, of forgiveness?

Martin Langford

From a train in Connecticut

Petrillo's Used Auto Parts just outside New Haven
contains about a thousand newish cars
all wrecked, rusting, with tyreless wheels
and cataracted windscreens.
There's not a soul in sight, just the river
flowing slowly in mild lobes
swapping one bank for another.
In his office sits Joe Petrillo, worried about his weight
and listening to the radio, sweating
on the Mets getting back their stars
in time for the playoffs.

Centuries ago near what became New Haven
the Quinnipiac and the Pequot fought a series of battles
or skirmishes, really, the Quinnipiac coming off second best,
eventually selling their land to some Europeans
in exchange for a peace of sorts.
Nearby, firs serry up a hill, just as near Munich,
where not as long ago there was a similar appeasement.
It's hard to imagine. It seems so peaceful here,
although the creeping greenery is an intimation
of violence, full of life and humid intent.

Last night Joe dreamt he'd killed his oldest friend,
years ago, and had been getting away with it all this time.
Awake, he remembers that he has not seen him
for several years now, not since the friend moved to Mystic, Connecticut.
Or was that a mistake? Perhaps
there's blood on his hands after all.
He can't be sure, now, in the wide hours
of early morning, unbalanced accounts
before him in a yet to be ordered pile.
This is the problem, not his business or his weight
but that he never seems to coincide
with himself. Whenever he finds himself,
it's always provisional, like a ford
in a rising river. Most of all he is afraid.
The blinded sun lights up,
serrates his thin Brancusi tube of smoke.

David Musgrave

Death by Dissonance

The NSW Government's Biosecurity unit is introducing a Pest Control order to prohibit the keeping of 'a newly acquired fox'

Part of his brain hates foxes,
hates the people who rescue,
neuter and vacc fox young, give
them to sensible homes, part
of his brain knows this
would make his synapses eschew
the crusade and relive
a time before poison, a whole heart
not patronised by a purity
in which all confusing mercy
is his non-native death.

Jennifer Maiden

boxing day test

twelfth man leaves the field
we tumble back to our places
sitting cross-legged
below a semicircle of lanky-shinned uncles
men, exhausted by another year's hard labour
and christmas day.

our skin sticks to itself
on boxing day in new south wales
the geography of each body irrigated by sweat
it is impossible to imagine standing outside
for each over and over again
cork and willow clap in the dry summer heat
of another state.

our uncles lean into the room
lean forward towards the box, as if they were next bat
tensing muscles deep in bare red-browned arms
they are in the memory position
revisiting lives they dreamed as boys
when they could imagine up a roaring crowd
that would lift them high above the drudgery
of normal men.

Cecilia White

Meeting the Relatives

They're on you before you know it,
careering around the corner in that
flashy ball of light – curious, energetic
and eager to share the fun. You're it.
Is that really you lying by the television or
slumped in the front seat, still alive?
You reach for a phone to call your mother
but she's saying don't worry darling,
I'm here, peeling away from your astonished
face another translucent mica flake.
There are layers of faces within you now,
each one vibrant with self-determined life,
fascinated by your stories, waiting their
turn to speak. You settle back painlessly
knowing the news can't be all bad, it's past!
These people you're descended from, who seem to
know you, are saying that they own you
as you float on your back in the champagne,
their faces are thought bubbles, popping
through your elevated, delighting brain.
A voice deep inside you, which could
be your own, is saying 'Let's go…'

Richard Tipping

The Fridge is Pregnant

The fridge is pregnant, it's about to give birth, there's people starving all over the earth, the fridge is a useful tool and the fridge is far too full. I'd love a cucumber sandwich, if I could get my mouth around it, I'd eat a hazelnut yoghurt, if it doesn't dribble down my T-shirt. The fridge is pregnant, it's about to give birth, there's people dying all over the earth, the fridge has a door that pulls and the fridge is far too full. I'd need to wash this down, all this food that I've found, I rummage in the shelves and I forage and I need a glass of orange. The fridge is pregnant, it's about to give birth, there's people dying all over the earth, the fridge makes my mouth drool and the fridge is far too full. Without you humming in the kitchen, there's bound to be something missing, it's great in the middle of the night, when you shine your white bright light. The fridge is pregnant, it's about to give birth, there's people dying all over the earth, the fridge keeps my food cool and the fridge is far too full.

Dan Eggs

Pārvatī in Darlinghurst

So I lay on the body of a pale Śiva. He spoke
not a word, bothered perhaps by my nut-brown
skin, my slow dance calmed his electro shuffle.
A slap of limbs pinned him down to my earth.
I hadn't bathed in sandalwood, flouting legend
with a preference for Estée Lauder. The moon's
crescent tangled my hair, my breasts were bare,
our timing synchronised. Night fizzed, vanishing
into day, the club's hypnotic rhythms subdued.
We scorned the Puranas, our tryst no Himalayan
cave, but a hotel bed I had draped with stockings,
lingerie, and the crystal ice of a Third Eye. I admit
that's why I spoke with the speed of an antelope.
It seemed the *acharyas* were mistaken: I hadn't
dated for marriage or adultery, nor with a wish
to deck his house with flowers or sweep his floors.
I am too busy, I declared, for dalliance or abstract
gossip. I have no interest in honeybees and birds.
All I wanted was a good time. I swear as the river
is my sister, that this guy was not my sun or my sky.
No way did it even enter my mind to have his kids.
His first wife's ashes were scattered all over the city.
Goddamn it, Śiva is a walking disaster; whatever
he touches burns. Restraining him with handcuffs
I said, 'Listen babe, your lingam and my yoni are
made for one thing only, improper and unchaste.
It's little more than conjecture to think our sweaty
helix could ever be whole.' Then I offered to grind
and gyrate him silly, suspend our want indefinitely,
and he fell utterly silent with this new meaning.

Michelle Cahill

Forgotten Nectar in the Sleeper's Cave

I will wake up to poetry once more
in a season aeons hence
kicking at a glow in the embers
to start one last fire
against the chill of my days

I will know in my bones
as I scratch out a few precious lines
that great poetry is immortal
it gets lodged
into the texture of our being

becomes part of the fabric
of who we are
and is there when we need it
like the memory of our first kiss
that moment

when we tasted
in that wet and sparkling fuse
in that dewy firecracker
a few flashing drops
from the blazing river of the soul

Richard James Allen

Poetry and Presenting it in Public
Part One

Is there different poetry for the 'stage' and the 'page' respectively?

Scott Sandwich: There is definitely a difference for me, but that's because I have more fun directly communicating with an audience. I'm still working on capturing that energy on the page, or at least the bits that I enjoy most about performance. Another reason I know there is a difference is because the works I love performing live are rarely enjoyable for me to read. This doesn't seem to be a problem for some of my favourite writers, but they're all better than me! It probably comes down to the fact that when you're looking at a poem, you have time and the chance to read and re-read and think about it, and to discover more each time. I'm not at the stage where I'm happy if people don't enjoy every sentence I utter. Having said that, I still leave surprises for second-time audiences.

Phil Radmall: Poetry for the stage, if you mean performance poetry, like anything heard, passes through and is gone, so there is an element of distance from the poem once it has been heard. Poems that are to be effective here should probably have a more direct intellectual and emotional impact. For the page, one can re-read, so the poem can be denser in meaning, not always obvious the first time – although still felt as something, even if not understood as something intellectually. But this is not to devalue either.

Cathy Bray: There is poetry that doesn't need to be read out to have the full impact that the poet intended. There is other poetry that only has the intended impact when it is read aloud – or benefits tremendously from having an audience.

Paul Buckberry: I don't think there should be (any difference).

I subscribe to the Clive James principle: 'I write as I sound and I sound as I write.'

Benito di Fonzo: Is there a difference? Yes and no. I think all writing should work read aloud, after all that's the great test of it. However, performance poetry/spoken word can be as much a form of miniature theatre as it can be literature. Rhythm, tone, word play, onomatopoeia – all take on extra importance. On top of that, the skills of public speaking come into play – humour, projection, timing. We must remember that poetry was originally an oral form. There is an argument that it's only when it became page-based that it distanced itself from the storytelling tradition that was at its root. All art is storytelling essentially. At its best, poetry read aloud can be a kind of music too. That said, poets like Jack Kerouac could write work that worked in both media. He's hard to book for a gig these days, though.

Les Wicks: Is there a difference? Yes and no. There is a spectrum with poems at one end that really don't fit the other medium.

Kate Lilley: There can be [a difference] but poetry that is difficult to read for various reasons can still be performed in some fashion.

David Falcon: When people hear a poem without being able to read it, they face additional challenges. I choose my poems for the stage with those challenges in mind. Foremost among them is the transient moment in which listeners have to form an image in their mind. Therefore, timing becomes important. It is best that the images are put forward slowly and built upon. As well, there are often pleasures to be drawn from written text which are not available to listeners. These can be sight rhymes or formations on the page.

William Tibben: Some poems work better than others read aloud. A reading [aloud] poem tends to be more direct and 'easier' in that sense, tends to like strong 'music' and aural features, tends to like clear, structural features – ballads, choruses and so on; tends to like humour, tends to need to be instant.

Martin Langford: There is much overlap, but there are also differences – some dense or allusive styles are impossible to follow in a single pass; the page allows one to check anything one didn't get.

Candy Royalle: Most poetry employs techniques that make it most beautiful when read aloud; therefore, page poetry should be read aloud, making it a perfect fit for the stage. Stage poetry should be as beautifully crafted as page poetry, so that it can be enjoyed in solitary silent moments. I don't believe there should be a difference between them.

Ed Wilson: There are obvious differences – with performance poetry being so much more '*Countdown* 1980s'; that is, being more 'rock and roll', gaudy and flamboyant – like a fellow who used to recite while swinging from the rafters at the Rail at Byron Bay – when I only remember the activity but not the poems. Singing or chanting usually enhances [such] presentations, with the profound emotionality that only music can evoke – emotions being the high-octane fuel of poetry. But on the page such 'poems' can be [seen] as rather thin, with blatant rhymes that can nudge banality. This problem, paradoxically, is diminished when overlaid with music… With my advancing years, this Grumpy Old Man can now admit to a special dislike of rap poetry. I cringe at the use of inane, repetitive and exceedingly unsubtle rhyme, a 'gangster-rock' equivalent to the Nashville twang in Australian country music. It is so obviously an American cultural import, not part of our own rich and independent old-Australian style, as we head down a road towards some bland, trans-Pacific, cultural 'unisex'. Page poetry is so much more 'dense' in imagery and contents – and generally more 'cerebral', not necessarily something that can be taken in aurally at the one performance.

Richard James Allen: I spent many years exploring this question – reading page poems, creating performance poems, mixing poetry and dance, creating character voices, writing dramatic monologues, then dialogues, performance texts and plays… The work of my first company, That Was Fast, directed with Karen Pearlman from 1985 to 1995, is a virtual catalogue of these experiments. My conclusion is that there is no simple answer to this question, only a spectrum of possibilities. But having been through all that, I also have to believe that a great poem for the page can be read [out loud] effectively. My horror with performance poetry has been the pressure that one can feel from outside and from within to dumb it down, to turn it solely into stand-up comedy.

Erwin Zehentner: It is only when you see an accomplished performer read work that you realise the difference. The intonation, use of negative spaces, timing of pauses and body language transform a modest offering into something special.

Do you prefer to introduce your poems before you read/perform them?

Scott Sandwich: You don't show the trailer for a film just before the movie starts. Your audience is already there, so trust them. If you need another way to think about it: good theatre is crafting it in such a way that the audience shouldn't have to read up on it just to understand it…but, of course, if they want to find out more, they can! It can still be abstract, it can still be weird, but if they (the audience) leave saying they understood nothing, then that's your fault, not theirs.

Phil Radmall: I would say yes, although only briefly. I hate the idea of a full contextual preamble. The poem should stand for itself.

Cathy Bray: Absolutely! I cling to the Federico Garcia Lorca defence – he said in his collection *Poet in New York* that he did not want his audiences to hear his poems cold. He wanted to give his listeners (often over a thousand people at a time) the background to each poem so that they could understand the complex metaphors and rhythms of his poems. This is in complete opposition to the attitude of the majority of established poets and academics in Sydney – the belief that all poems should stand alone, never requiring any explanation or introduction.

Paul Buckberry: It's a question of time and place and mood. Some poems need no introduction.

Susan Adams: Depends on the event.

Kate Lilley: Not usually – but I'm happy to if asked.

Les Wicks: Context, context – some poems need it. It can build a rapport with the audience. But neophyte readers often fall foul of allowing their nervousness to lead to [intro] babble.

Benito di Fonzo: Generally, I'd say it's a bad idea to introduce a poem, unless that is part of the performance. If the title is so great you really need to say it, then do so, or better still add it to the poem! But it can be annoying when somebody spends as long, or longer, introducing a poem as reading the poem itself. Let the poem do the work – it's a little play, let them get it. Don't patronise the audience, they're not all idiots.

Candy Royalle: I like the work to do its own storytelling.

Richard James Allen: Sometimes an introduction is what is needed. Sometimes just launching into it. Sometimes something else unexpected.

William Tibben: Most poems benefit from some intro, but it's a fine line. It could be argued that if it's good enough it shouldn't need an intro.

Martin Langford: Part of the sharpness – and power – of verse lies in incorporating only the minimum amount of contextualisation: a reader can take his or her time over this, but if the audience doesn't enter the poem with the speaker, it's lost. That said, intros should be minimal only. It is, however, a mistake to say, 'If a poem is any good, it doesn't need an introduction.' Some do, some don't.

Edwin Wilson: I generally prefer to introduce a poem – to hopefully put myself and my audience more at ease. A little preamble puts everyone in a better space (to enjoy the reading).

David Falcon: I do prefer to introduce my poems and also prefer that the poems I'm hearing have some introduction. However, it must be interesting and have relevance. If the introduction is no more than a self-indulgent description of the poet's epiphanic moment ,it is better not done.

Erwin Zehentner: I think it is important to give some introduction to some work.

Why do you want to read your poems to others?

Benito di Fonzo: Beats laying bricks! Also, good writing is like music, and you can get in the pocket and flow. Storytelling is part of what makes us human. Writing is storytelling. As I said earlier, reading it aloud is the ultimate test. Also, it helps sell books, and poets…

Cathy Bray: Because I have something to say and no other way to say it.

Les Wicks: Poetry is so challenged in most countries I feel the poet has an obligation to access every possible channel of dissemination.

Scott Sandwich: It's really really fun. I'm not terribly complex.

Paul Buckberry: To communicate relatable thoughts and feelings and possibly help listeners appreciate a different understanding of something familiar.

Phil Radmall: Despite what I said in question 1, there is an art to speaking a poem 'to' someone – as opposed to 'at' someone – and this can benefit a poem that sounds well on the ear as well as on the eye. I think people like to see a poet read their poems; gives them flesh and bone to relate to.

Susan Adams: To familiarise them (the audience) with me – the poet – and present my work.

Candy Royalle: I believe that shared pain makes the load lighter, shared joy increases that joy. A collective experience of sharing stories, listening, engaging with each other makes life more rich. Additionally, I believe, in a world as stifling, corrupted and disjointed as ours, we need a diversity of voices (and views) to combat it.

Edwin Wilson: There are times during poetry readings – with a receptive, warmed-up crowd – usually when reacting to the unexpected serendipities of other readings to some particular theme, when there is so much anticipation in the room that the air almost crackles with static charge, and bright sparks tap and release this energy in the form of wit, and bounce ideas, and people laugh, and that's when a certain magic happens, when the stars and planets and the elements are somehow all aligned.

Richard James Allen: There is joy in sharing what you do. Feeling the response. Being in a circle of communication. With an increasingly mediated society, I think audiences will be drawn back more and more to the immediacy, intimacy and visceralness of live performance. And also its unexpected, unscripted aspects. In the moment of performance, you can bring one reading of a work into life, to inhabit that fully. On another occasion, you might explore another petrson's reading. And these live performances of the text don't take away from the experience of a reader interpreting the text for themselves. They will also find different things each time they return. A truly profound text is, in Roland Barthes' terms, inexhaustible, irreducible.

Kate Lilley: I enjoy reading aloud and the sense of immediate response. I also enjoy putting together groups of poems/groups of poets for readings.

David Falcon: I get pleasure from it and I think it's the same pleasure you get out of giving a gift. When I hear a poem, I really like it comes to me like something shared and generously given. It is a beautiful sharing of what it is to be human. When I read my poems publicly, I am consciously trying to do that for my audience.

Erwin Zehentner: There is a Porky Pig in all of us and a good dose of Ham sandwiches enhances any reading. It is an 'I can do this too' thing. Notice how kids often naturally recite rhymes among their group.

Martin Langford: Why do I want to read my poems to an audience? Because a poem is not complete until an audience – or readership – dances with it too. Because reading it out does add an extra dimension – the bodily one – to the poem's meaning.

Willem Tibben: In one sense, a poem is not a poem until it has been heard/read by others. More importantly for me, hearing one's work aloud before an audience highlights the cringe spots – did I really write that? Reading in front of others strips away a lot of the poem's preciousness and pretension – or, conversely, really brings it cringingly out! You stand vulnerable, clothed only in rags of language – there you go.

2007

Louise Oxley from Tasmania was our first special guest, along with David Mulligan (better known to Live Poets regulars as actor and poet David Morris). We opened the year to a satisfying audience roll-up.

Louise's words made daring etchings of love in the country against a mother's advice; passion in remote landscapes generating tension and impatient echoes behind that boy in the bush. In other poems, her elegant language was rooted in depiction of the natural world. Louise also gave an excellent interview (the final applause of a couple of dozen people positively thundered).

David has taken to writing fiction for younger readers centred on real events. *Angels of Kokoda* honours the help the local fuzz-wuzzy angels lent the Australian World War II effort in Papua New Guinea. (A book on the Rats of Tobruk is next up). These books are designed to make the younger generation more familiar with iconic moments of our history as a white nation. David's actor's voice teased out the nuances, choreographing the drama to acclaim in response – so that we all rediscovered things we thought we knew. David's interview was peppered with wry commentary on 'the agent of a book contract directs his lackey at the wheel' style. The sales figures are already good.

The publicity and distribution afforded by a large publisher makes so much difference. And contrasted with the fate that recently met Chris Broadrib's novel launched at the NSW Writers Centre – which she read from at Don Bank this night. Matt Moore was there to lend his inimitable take on the spoken word scene and talk about his ambition to set up an effective Sydney Writers website with a zany pop edge.

In March there were six featured guests! Margaret Bradstock, Kerry Leves, Joanna Burns, Jenni Nixon, David Musgrave and

Louise Wakeling presenting Poems in Conversation, which I'd seen earlier performed in Parramatta. This show featured poems from different voices speaking to each other, as Musgrave apparently once reported his poems responding to those of Bradstock. Propelled by an engaging article in the *Mosman Daily*, the night was solidly supported.

There were new voices among the open section line-up including a young Maori girl, Kiko. (Her parents questioned this convenor on the nature of his business as he rang to remind Kiko, 'It's on this Wednesday'!)

Our April meeting fell on the actual Anzac Day holiday and was not illogically entitled 'The Question of War'. The floor was thrown open to poetic or musical responses to this question. This convenor opened proceedings in a darkened room with an a cappella version of Don McLean's 'The Grave' – torchlight held under the chin showing just the mouth as he intoned.

People were able to go round twice – before and after supper of tea and damper. The supplied content followed a history of war starting with the Spartans and the Tamil Kings through to Peter Porter's address to a nation on the cusp of a nuclear attack – 'Attention Please'. Margaret Vermuch offered a searing eyewitness account of the Third World War. There was a reporter present from the *North Shore Times*.

The proximity of May meetings of Live Poets to events from the Big End of Town (the SWF) can often be a problem, deterring people from attending Don Bank. I once asked John Kinsella if he would like to do a reading at Live Poets because he was in town for the Writers Festival and he replied he'd love to but his SWF contract forbade it.

This year by contrast, the May meeting produced our best gate outside of venue birthday celebrations for some years. A clue to that was the great response the local paper received after its story on the night's guests: Michelle Cahill and Kate Waterhouse. The writer of the story cited Michelle's normal occupation as a local GP as the reason. Who can resist a doctor who prescribes poetry?

Michelle in her interview at Don Bank denied that was how it worked – the two parts of her life are strictly divided! She could have said three parts, for Michelle is also the editor of the online poetry magazine *Mascara* – no, not an Elizabeth Arden catalogue! – that is steadily gathering strength, opening the doors of poetry and writings from other countries – particularly Asia and the Pacific Rim. This is not only a boom area economically. Michelle's poetry covers a wide range of subjects – she offered several rich examples after her interview.

Kate Waterhouse, originally from New Zealand, would have been far less known but, on the strength of her engaging interview and a reading of tenderness, comedy and clarity here, she will rapidly remedy that. Then you read the book and you discover the poems come off even better on the page! Interestingly, the teenage son of *Mosman Daily* reporter Kate Crawford, Darcy, was dropped off at Don Bank this night to witness a poetry event for the first time – and what a crowded house to lose yourself in!

A promising young poet, Jacob Ziguras, opened the proceedings of a huge open section. Jim Low, down from the mountains. offered some songs. Vicki Watson was a first-timer with 'how music affects me during writer's block'. Tom Thorpe offered a wonderful play on words involving town's names: 'Why didn't we dwell in Piddle in Creek?' Mark Hislop wittily observed, 'All the girls have sat down tonight and the guys have stood.' Moree Ward was back after a long time away, as lovably sarcastic as ever! This convenor closed the evening with 'Faun and Minotaur', where the bull-man subject of a Picasso etching talks.

Ketut Yuliarsa from Indonesia was the special guest for June.

He brought along an important companion – a mask which he left on the front table after his reading with the challenge, 'People coming up to read after me are welcome to try on this mask and see what voice it lends them.' Masks form an important part of Balinese religion and culture, helping the wearer evoke another identity. People feel freer wearing a mask. It invites the reader to join the audience in a communal trancing. The power in that action can change lives and influence the consciousness of whole villages in Indonesia. Would the shaman 'in' the mask run amok in the Don Bank sitting room? The risk was there to be accepted or not.

Many poets, of course, wear many different masks every day and have to do that to access their creativity or ability to dissemble, to live several realities at once. Philip Larkin in the library and T.S. Eliot in the bank are two of the most important examples from history. Those realities become periodically friable and combustible as they rub against each other – like at a poetry reading.

Ketut was reading from his latest book, *Sita's Poems*, which had its background in the fabled Ramayama legend. His last poem featured 'Noah's Ark' (in the time of the 2004 tsunami in Aceh). Ketut, who runs a bookshop in his other life in Bali and a publishing company striving to keep alive the island's original Bahasa tongue, spoke of Bali's tiny stature as a Hindu island in the vast archipelago of Muslim Indonesia and the struggle in the consciousness of Bali's youth between the old traditions and the pressures of the modern world. 'They are more ready to face these issues armed with the traditional strengths – but the future is uncertain.' Ketut is not only a poet. He's worked in theatre and film here and in Indonesia. His poems have been set to music by Paul Grabowsky for an Adelaide Festival program. He has an Australian wife.

Ketut's son Jonah was also at Don Bank and delivered a

poem about a James Cook statue.

Bill Tibben was one open section poet who tried on Ketut's mask as he read his piece called 'Albert and Vincent' – a clash of opposites. There was music from regular Paul Buckberry and Jessica Morgan – out here from the USA – who didn't project strongly but I hope she comes back. Pip Griffin read from her latest book, *The Journey of a Monk (across Burma)*. Danny L offered three elliptical pieces translated from the Czech.

Poetry is really the largest club in the world – we owe it such a debt in its enrichment of our life.

In July, Live Poets hosted three poets from Iraq – Fadeel Kayat, Mohsen Beni Saeed and Jamal al Hallaq. These men had presented Writing on Gravestones at the Sydney Writers Festival last year with Dharfur Kadeer, crowding out the Bangarra Mezzanine and inspiring onlookers with their frank, defiant humour.

I set up a meeting with Jamal and Mohsen in the city before their appearance at Don Bank to try and get to the nub of Arabic conventions in producing poetry. It seemed to be concerned with small effects in the frame of large networks. The elements often played the role of a character in the human action trying to decide whether to aid him or hinder; a certain fatalistic outcome tended to obtain. Nevertheless, the humans talked to this over-riding force, treating it like a brother, an ally or a foe according to context. I had a particular theory about its affect but I was swiftly assured it was generated by conventions of Arabic poetry, as translated into English! It was the eternal conundrum!

Jamal the poet and Mohsen the translator form a double act. They remind you of a couple of businessmen – replete with formal suits – offering the audience a deal! The interplay between them was so quick and sharp, often with the persuasive pacing of a sort of comedy routine. Jamal, for instance, would murmur a few lines into space and Mohsen with a quizzical expression would shortly reveal to us, 'It's okay, he's only – he hasn't started yet!'

There was one hilarious piece of Jamal's where he wishes to stop time, unravel his life and start afresh and his forebears apparently wish it too. It starts with 'My mother…wants her womb back.' Mohsen's deadpan interpreting was always dovetailing delightfully with Jamal's meditative earnestness. The Don Bank crowd couldn't get enough.

Fadeel, moreover, descendant of the Marsh Arabs Saddam Hussein sought to exterminate, was the quintessential lone wolf survivor, as it appeared in English; master of the exacting, almost journalistic unpeeling of an onion in such works as: 'All in One', 'Public Tree', 'To Bob Dylan' and 'To T.S. Eliot'. A marvellous counterpoint therefore to the 'Blues Brothers' Mohsen and Jamal, though of course they had their quiet, telling moments too.

Whether she designed it that way or not I'm not sure, but the second poem from Jenny Campbell coming on after the Iraqi poets was 'Barbaric Grist', which told of witnessing Saddam Hussein's execution in Baghdad. Matthew Moore meantime wanted to conquer the world as a Dalek. He'd debuted this poem originally to his workmates at a city investment firm.

The program for August was entitled Yesterday's Warning: Global Warming and Climate Change. How should we (as poets) respond?

The special guest for this was singer/guitarist Paul Buckberry. After three songs by Paul to start, this convenor did 'Parliament Bar' with the refrain 'We Have to Set Targets? What do you want to do – destroy our way of life?' There was a poem each by Les Wicks ('swimming in July') and Moree Ward, Danny Lovecraft's

'Big Feet: a mystery', Pip and Penelope with a ditty on the issue.

Three more songs by Paul came next, ending with the emblematic 'White Skin'. After supper, Paul did three more tunes, ending with 'Flash News Flash'. Then came Bee Perusco with a wistful a cappella, 'Simon' (a creepy rework of *1984*) and Moy Hitchens' 'God Made Us Trees'. Paul B almost took us to the end with 'Earth Hour' and this convenor finished with 'Earth Rise': the Apollo 9 astronauts contemplating a new home planet on their way back from the moon. This was of course very early days on this issue (still not early enough), but there seemed plenty of hope and energy on tap to tackle our fossil fuel and black discharge obsessions under Uncle Kevin.

September was mostly music. Ben Ezra with his hip-hop urban mythologising – the biting ballad about Sleepy Hollow, the scene of razor gang warfare in Surry Hills in 1930, for instance – raised significant questions. Why do remakes of American classics from Basin Street to the Wichita Lineman and untold Dylan clone tunes when a rich source of Australian legendary places and events are right under our feet? Ben had prefaced the 1930s classic with a riveting cameo of a 'stand up broken Swan (a beautiful and destroyed inmate) at Callan Park' and the elegiac 'Down to You'. There were some brief burning words from the 'urban gringo, blues gonzo' as well before Ezra had to cut out to the city for another gig. The set left almost everyone a bit stunned. 'A real presence,' one person commented. 'Surely this guy has a CD out there,' others said. He's destined to make a lot of other hip-hops own up to inadequacies, I believe.

After supper it was time for Live Poets' favourite chanteuse – Kate Maclurcan – to wow us anew with a playlist of: 'Grandfather', 'Everest Eyes', 'Bright Red Car', 'The Howard Times (a liar, a bore)', Eric Bogle's 'White, Anglo-Saxon Middle-aged Male', 'Sunday Morning Coming Down', a standard, and 'Our Town'.

This convenor later read out Ezra's poem from *Light on Don Bank* – 'Hobo Atlas' – in his wake. Bill T told of a lobster in a Stanley (Tassy) pub. Danny Lovecraft aired two pieces from the book, *Ramblings of an Attic Mind*.

Bill Tibben was the man in charge in October as this convenor was away climbing Mount Kiliminjaro. Caroline Gerrish was the guest – a woman who felt laughter was the saviour of mankind and Australia would be better off with the Chaser gang (from ABC TV fame) in charge. By all accounts it was a pleasant evening with the usual smattering of regulars and fans of Gerrish's from Balmain on hand. She read from her book of poems, *Dark Laughter*. Carolyn teaches creative writing at WEA. Her work has been described as an ironic/lyrical exploration of the self in contemporary society.

For November we had the poetry of Professor of English at Sydney Uni, David Brooks, and the songs of NZ-born singer/guitarist Wayne Gillespie.

David combined an ironic take on urban living with meditations on space and the elements – the view out the back porch which we hope never changes. Lately, a more urgent, environmental concern has been encroaching. David cited his second book, *Walking to Point Clear*, as the first stage in this process. It's been accelerated through David's succeeding books of fiction and poetry but the poetry is more 'up to date on it'.

David has taught several people who were in the audience that night, including one Chris Raft, who was chastised at this meeting for his poems being 'offensive to a forum of good poetry' – a claim later put into writing to this convenor. David straight-batted a gentle bit of heckling from the recalcitrant Mr Rath.

Wayne Gillespie is yet another fine singer/songwriter who has come to earth over the last couple of years in Sydney and entertained with wry and gnarly (*the* adjective of 2007?) urban blues – particularly the self-excoriating 'Geriatric Blues'. Wayne had been doing this at a busk recently (as he related) and had a ten-franc note 'dropped into my pail by a Leonard Cohen look-a-like in an overcoat.' To which Wayne responded automatically with a swing into 'Hey that's no way…to say goodbye!'

Afterwards, Stuart Howard read 'Life is Fine', a poem by Afro-American Langston Hughes.

This convenor had opened the show with a quote from the King of Texcoco in pre-Cortés central Mexico: 'We come here only to sleep, to dream. We did not come to live on this earth. Our body is a plant in flower. It gives up its blossom and dies away.'

We closed with an announcement of the annual UnDarwin Awards to people who have enriched our lives in 2007. The special guests at Live Poets got the gong of course.

Listening for the road

A rush of wind through the big radiata
sounds like your Renault on the gravel,
like you returning, calmer,
clouds of spent anger settling behind you.
It sounds like you driving down the hill
towards the house where I sit in late sun
with wine and poems on the garden bench
we assembled only yesterday,
looking up to the road from time to time,
to the massive pine, its needles seething,
its branches swaying like resolve,
between gusts going quiet.
Wrens fan out across the grass
like a search party. The sea breeze goes on
entering the tree and leaving it,
which is the sound of you
not rounding the gravel bends, not coming.

Louise Oxley

salon

stainless steel in a homburg hat
sucked on that giant cigar on the top
floor of the double-decker bus before
it lurched into the view where the road
curved past the sleepy cop shop, years
before the view was appellated into 'the
view', before the bay was dredged of its
low-tide stench   cigar smoke rose
through a passenger's nostrils higher
than rumours of papal ash   as the transport
lurched and accelerated portmanteaux flew onto
the road like bulky archives or death duty files – the
man in the brown suit near the chic salon stood there
all afternoon, the long scar on his left cheek waiting for
a crime movie yet to be made   those lost to a ritual
of spelling bee glory had little idea of a greater prize

joanne burns

White, Whitely, Whitest

'a face left wondering whether truth can be the greatest destroyer of all' – Patrick White, *Flaws in the Glass*
after Brett Whitely, *Portrait of Patrick White at Centennial Park*, 1979–80

White, salient one, baleful stare of a newly-minted zombie, loose-armed
and boneless in his chair, likes dogs without collars, hates the overgrown
school prefects we're lumbered with in public life: *verboten* lists of likes
and hates legible to all: even today, we tie ourselves in knots to read them
in the gallery (though who could argue with that, watching
the latest politicians twist and turn in the wind?)

the whole thing a collage of Brett himself, nothing literally true, 'The House',
bone-white claws   scratched us awake, teeth of the Great White bit us
into consciousness, artist and icon introducing a new continent to itself.
And no sprinkler in the front garden, no bird-feeder, the wrong aspect
from Centennial Park, where they walked – young man, old man,
companionable, the view east, not north – even Manoly, calm and kindly –

a satyr-faced Significant Other leering from a frame, owlish,
vaudeville, like one of the Marx brothers…what was that about?
And a sprawling erotic magnolia – a cluster of pistils clutched by stamens,
image lifted from another work, androgynous, Brett the wild young artist

drunk on White's chaise longue after boozy dinners, taken up, at first, a delight,
an odalisque – idolised, tolerated, dropped. The charge: dishonesty, betrayal.
White, furious. Never liked being snagged on another man's 'truth'.
The artist deleted the exchange.   Like it never happened.

Louise Wakeling

November Evening – Nottingham Castle

for Stu whose hair was wet

Soft fell the rain
and ran in rivulets
between the cobblestones.
Colourfully opaque the sky
an exotic opal
tinged by the half-reflected lights
of the city.

Before us, steep-rising
the sandstone
a massive dark-hued face
of weather-patterned rock.
A backcloth transcending time
against which, silhouetted
a cavalcade of knights, foresters
cavaliers and portly laughing friars
moved, swelled organ-like, and
faded out of focus.

Soft fell the rain
a crystalline sparkle
of raindrops on your hair
brushed cold against my face.
And soft fell the rain.

Thomas Thorpe

Polling Day

I left the voting booth with the pencil dangling on its string
twitching at the last
like the incumbent government

and folded my vote like an origami of
a misshapen, sinking ship of state
and fed it into the large box full of them

so much paper: enough perhaps
for a White Paper, then I

went up the road for a Chinese.
I could hardly see the maggots
for the long grain, still thinking of

this one's policy on the boats
and that one's

The rice here's never soggy

Bob Howe

Stranded Noah's Ark

The Noah's Ark which has left the last doomsday
is yet to arrive here, perhaps it has been trapped and stranded
in the gap of time.
It could also have been lost in the vastness of the universe, for
the old master's vision
could have been obscured by the mist surrounding the sea.

So there's no place to hide from these falling buildings
the sky roars with exploded rockets spreading poisonous gas.
There is nothing to hold onto when wild waves crash
to drown our cry, burying our pain, wiping out villages instantly.
Only from the distance survivors can be heard
urging us to continue the voyage toward a sorrowless isle.

Maybe Noah's Ark has landed
beyond this material world, to welcome
millions of souls, the victims of natural disasters
lining up from one era to another.

Perhaps now, the time is right
to open the bottle with the message
for it has been too long sealed in secrecy
perhaps our names are inscribed in there
chosen to embark on the everlasting journey.

Ketut Yuliarsa

By the river

They sat by the river
And talked about
Everything
– Other than the weather.
The light dancing on water
The mountain that reminded them of home
Trees bleeding like women
Favourite lines of poems
Often, God was the one who took the third seat.
She said He was there, he wasn't so sure.

They walked by the river
And cried over
People who had come and gone
But not gone completely
Places they had been
That brought them to this moment
And secrets that had made motifs in their hearts
Motifs too complex to share with the world were divulged
Like an Ottoman rose – petal by petal
By their river, time stood still and they swam in its expanse

They swam in the river
As they waited for each other
To be free.

Isil Cosar

Public Tree

I leave my hand on a tree
that you may
one day lay your hand
on that tree.

I leave my eyes
in a book
that you may one day
open your eyes in that book

I leave my lips
on a cup in a pub
that you may one day
run your lips on that cup

I bow to every stone
that you may have once walked by
or one day you may walk
by that stone.

Fadeel Kayat

Mama Named Her Paris France

Where *The Wonder Years* meets *Breaking Bad*,
Mama's little girl lived with her muddled-up Dad.
She grew up poor, starved for affection,
So poor that girl couldn't pay attention.

Mama named her Paris France.
She said, 'Leaving these hills is my only chance.'
Hopped the Mount Vic train in a cold March rain,
Skyped her friends across the river Seine.

'Sisters three don't weep for me.
Mountains blue, my soul set free'
Her status says:
Paris is half the world away.

Met the Judas Davy near the grey old arch,
All alone down the Champs dancing in the dark.
The warmth he gave her made her lazy
Till all she needed was the Judas Davy.

Spoke to the police, doctor and priest,
Chose Judas over reality and peace.
Judas in Paris' eyes and mouth,
Judas in Paris and it all points south.

'Sisters three don't weep for me.
Mountains blue, my soul set free'
The rain stops and starts.
Paris has broken a thousand hearts.

An endless day, a clock hand turning,
A spoon and a candle with both ends burning.
In the tidal wave of dreams, in her final hour,
Every wizard, witch and fiend had power.

Those Paris hotel walls are peeling,
She stared at the crack across the ceiling.
We know how she died and know how she lived
But it ain't what you gain it's what you give.

See a million stars across a purple sky,
See one fall right before your eyes.
From the dangers of the darkness it bursts so bright
Then disappears forever into endless night.

'Sisters three don't weep for me.
Mountains blue, my soul set free'
There but for the grace…
Paris is in the most beautiful place.

Paul Buckberry

The Sea Dragon's Tale

I have a tale
A tale for you
Humans of our earth
Listen, it's true.

I give you my tale
To do what you'll do
A tale of my home
Destroyed by humans, like you.

Where I belong
My home in the sea
There has been
A catastrophe.

Our world is no longer
The world that we knew
We are now homeless, all
Humans what are we to do?

We creatures won't accept
That this can't change
This path need not be
You humans, you're strange.

We don't understand you
You're fearless, you're strong
We showed you our hand
And you did us wrong.

Now my life is lost
And I wander here
To save what is left
Of all I hold dear.

Don't ignore
The signs you see
Look at the sky, sun, moon
Earth and sea.

Take a look
Listen too
Is this not precious?
I ASK YOU.

Bee Perusco

Hauntings

they come calling   pawing at doors &
windows   let me in   i'm so cold   their
hoarse voices   mist from floorboards
ceilings & hallways   how to persuade a ghost
to move on   get a life   (exorcisms   so messy)
but they have a stake in shadowy perpetuation
& any lack of focus   from the living   can
encourage a bogeyman   **they**'re omnipresent
invisible at corporate meetings   hiding in the
powerpoint   able to alter the flexible past
& there   in the windless garden   a child's
swing   creaking back & forth   & a cadaver
emerges from the unlit café   phantom limb
kicks an empty crisps packet   onto the
noir street

& perhaps you need the shining   to apprehend
something so varied & wandering   that spectral
diaspora   unable to rest   **you** appear to be
human   but are quickly cut dead   by a friend
who walks away   waving to the anonymous air
& a clairvoyant shuffles/cuts cards   claims
intimacy with the underworld   someone who has
passed over   is with you   today

Carolyn Gerrish

2008

Live Poets started the new year with what I consider the optimum program for the venue – a special guest in poetry and unplugged music respectively.

Stephen Edgar has a lyrical structure to what doesn't always seem free verse. He says he's often in search of a subject and finds something else on the way! There is elegy and beauty and often surprising questions.

Pat Drummond is something of a local legend in North Sydney. He held his last gig on a Friday at the nearby Wrest Hotel for years! What he was on about was saving the venue (yet another live gig) from demolition. This fate hung over the Wrest's head in the courts until it became a social issue people voted on with their feet. Pat now says, 'It was one of those crazy things that happens. People took bits of the place home with them at the bitter end. A weird sort of revenge. I went on the road and inhabited various personas consequently.' I heard about a gigantic chess set that Pat built on stage every night as a site gag, Pat becoming a travelling reporter presenting his newcomer's view of the towns on his tours. I asked Pat about his role in the biggest-selling purveyors of poetry on disc – The Naked Poets. There was plenty of press interest in this gig at Don Bank because of Pat's local reputation. I had Pat's music on the PA as people were coming in.

Barbara Fisher and Miles Merrill meantime lent quality to the open section. Kate Maclurcan did a song of Pat's about the first refugee – Jesus. Danny Lockhart is now a publisher and he told us a little about P'rea Press. Tara offered a poem on the recently departed Heath Ledger (our very own James Dean): 'and a poem I made into a song at sixteen and was inspired by Pat and it's called "Old Man"'.

The unhappiest performer on the night was Yuri the Storyteller. He was infamous in Live Poets' early days for his stories and legends uttered in the light of his famous flickering candle. Genuinely chilling on occasion. I asked Yuri not to use the candle because of the stringent fire regulations around historic buildings these days that, if breached, could conceivably have us looking for another venue tomorrow. He insisted he had to use his candle. I said I would not ask him to read if that was the case. He decided he would read anyway – without the candle. I turned off some lights to help promote a shadowy effect. I only thought later that Yuri could have done a reading in the courtyard over supper – but we had a full program and were running late as it was. Yuri's story was about an Irish bridesmaid/mermaid who haunts a man hesitant and gullible towards apparent fortune. It was not Yuri's most polished appearance. 'That was probably the worst reading I've ever done! Thanks to your attitude. Who do you think you are? Joseph Goebbels?' Don't tell me – it must be February again!

In March, Peter Kirkpatrick arrived to take us back to Bohemia – a concept from Europe in the late nineteenth century which had its heyday Down Under in the 1970s. It's probably more famous for that soubriquet, 'You're nothing but a Bohemian!' A character trait more than a movement. A philosophy of free thinking and creative morals was how some people wore it. 'I'm old enough not to make guidelines for the role in poetry!' Peter offered. One of Peter's poems about the Mitchell Reading Room could be read as an epigram to libraries. His 'Phantom of the Opera' – a mashup of characters fleeing the tyranny of manners and social standing embodied bohemia as behaviour that is always present in literature somewhere.

Henry Sheerwater from Tasmania (he's been living there the last couple of years) rendered a superb performance – as much in the air as on the page; testaments to facing yourself alone and the role of poetry in conservation issues. Henry offered an engaging patter between poems too; his imitation of crow sounds at one point wrapped around us like an address out of silence. It was magical. Henry's father was in the audience and his eyes shone at the reception Henry received.

It was another good gate, with several first-timers. People were asked to comment on the PR poster of a blindfolded person at a typewriter pecking out dice and question marks – the fruit of his labour left up to chance. The figure is decidedly anonymous, a product of the Mechanical Generation dealing data – a kid could do that, a chimp could do that.

Danny Lockhart reflected on its message. 'What we are about to produce is not for us to know. The knife-marks in the back are souvenirs when you start out being Caesar!'

Frank Ezbury: 'It's a portrait of the doom we all fear.' He then proceeded to detail a soldier's nightmare and we suddenly realised (with audible gasps from some people) the soldier was Frank.

Jeremy: 'All part of the growing into the execution – having signalled the need.'

Simon, a man of few words generally, presented a suitcase novel full of characters from Tin Can to Veronica Wentworth to No-Name and Rats-Off, who then become subversive to gangsta rule.

With yet another birthday in April, there was a tribute to the late Vera Newsom's last book of collected poems, *Grace*. Vera was the special guest at our very first Live Poets Society meeting at the L'Orangerie Café, Neutral Bay, in April 1990. Vera became a poet in public at a late stage of her life. She only had twenty to thirty years free from family responsibility to write rather than the normal forty to fifty year span, so everything had to be 'caught – exact!' Vera admitted she often felt like an old woman preoccupied with a foreclosing future, yet simultaneously discovering a magic in life's detail.

Three esteemed local poets – Martin Langford, Martin Harrison and Anna Kerdjik Nicholson – took us through their experiences with Vera and read their favourites from *Grace* in a rich night of anecdote and verses as they happened.

Martin Langford: 'I'm a bit of a ring-in for this compared to Brook Emery say or Judith Beveridge, who were originally asked to do it. Vera did help me get a book of poems out and I worked with her like Anna did at Roundtable [Publications]. Vera was tiny in stature but a formidable human being. Certain English people (particularly women) have a reputation for being reserved but Vera had a keen reception of spirit and knew how to nail down meaning with lucidity and clarity. There's more than a little of the romantic in her too – you could imagine her being quite a fiery girl in her time. She was a feminist – a pivotal voice carried over from that generation born around the First World War, an enduring flame.'

Anna: 'We came from similar parts of England – Cumbria and North Yorkshire – and shared something of a sensibility though we were forty years apart in age. I got to know her over some whiskies in her green study in her Balmain apartment. Later she asked me to be her lawyer, take care of the matters of her passing. At Roundtable, I witnessed the exhausting focus she achieved while rewriting, honing, distilling and exemplifying the essence, as parts of poems had to be tortuously reworked. Poets become their poetry, their material and vice versa – with Vera much more than other writers. These fragments I will read are emblems of that indelible imperative Vera lent to words…'

Martin Harrison: 'It was entrancing for me – at twenty-five teaching Vera, at sixty-five, about writing [she was in Martin's class at UTS]. It was remarkable how, at her age, she could be so involved and be able to contribute so much to the work that the class achieved. She really despaired of being able to write at all sometimes…you can be a boat becalmed at any age but a late-aroused muse is ever so fickle. At those times, the world for Vera felt depthless and bereft. In the class, Vera was able to articulate the most extreme challenges surrounding her age and yet tackle the hard questions – I feel that's unique to a select group of poets in twentieth century Australian literature – Harwood, Wright, Giles and so on. In the end, doing this book [*Grace*] was painstaking – a single word could take so long because Vera's hand was shaking so much. Judith B and her were close. They needed things about each other. Over and over, Vera revised but she couldn't let something go until it was final, fixing that moment that wouldn't come again.'

Chris Raft's flute playing of 'Happy Birthday' in the courtyard had charmed the throng and his poem later was curse-free and struck a few telling chords. This convenor opened with 'Eye in the River Bends' ref Sydney Nolan's triptych of the Glenrowan constable catching Kelly in the awful glue-bog gloaming of remote country, and Moy Hitchen said, 'I saw that picture at the Art Gallery of NSW and wrote a poem about it too!' Erwin Zehentner read a poem of George Trakl's (a chemist by trade who died of a heroin overdose in 1914) and commented, 'There was this mountain where the water went. There was this man in a sanitorium who was quite a genius. It was my home town.'

In May, Jane Gibian was the guest. Shy and jokey by turns – she was a serious twenty-five-year old who seems younger, an inner-city girl liking but trying to be more comfortable with Bondi. It was a good interview. I'm finding it's often better to be more spontaneous – just wing it with the questions. The poems showed a fragility in Jane which she wants to offset with the tough intellect rigorously honing the words' shape.

Ron Wilkins read some poems about China. I had this flash – had he been there with Mary Tang? She had said after he had paid for them both to come in, 'Ah, OK, I'll get lunch!' Mary had just been accepted at a writers retreat in Bali – the final six places had been narrowed down from 700-plus entries. She complained about not reading till after supper and then took up a prepared portfolio (it turns out she'd mistakenly thought I'd okayed her for a guest spot!). I had to stop her after three poems. She sang the life of a lady in the Kimberleys as though it was her second skin.

Another reader had given his name at the door as Garrick Hooper and we laughed about *High Noon* and he said, 'No, I haven't got my spurs on!' as he came up to deliver.

In June, we had that one poet and one musician guest regime again – with Craig Powell and Kate Fagan – though Kate can also write the odd verse! There was another healthy crowd in attendance. Craig is something of a raconteur; his golden tones are ideal for disseminating a lyric. His was a rich generous performance, but difficult to bring to a close.

Supper arrived late with Helen, but we were even later. No one wanted Craig to finish – what could I do? Kate's family, the Fagans, were originally English from Northumberland. They have carved out their own mythology in Australian folk music. Kate carries the flame eloquently – the voice ringing clear through verse and melody, and her picking is sublime. Really she could have carried the evening herself – poems one side of supper, songs and album notes the other.

Of the open section readers, Bhuppen Thakker was a fire-starter with his 'Doesn't anyone love anyone else any more?' and 'I live on 5 dollars a day versus I live on a 1,000 dollars a day'.

Robert Kennedy, organiser of the poetry group Diverse, that give readings in galleries responding to the artworks therein, broke out with some fine examples. Diverse could make a good guest feature in the future.

July was something of a New Zealand night. Ross Hattaway lives in Ireland now but was originally from the Shaky Isles. Pip Griffin has lived many years in Sydney after coming across the ditch. Penelope Grace offered up some fiddle to get the fire started.

In the interview about his book *Gentle Art of Rotting*, Ross contended, 'Humans are not very good at many things – have to wander around to find actions they can join in. They also have to rot their food so they can digest it properly – a clever idea to base a poem on? Maybe. Now there are countless titles coming out about this and stealing my idea!' Ross's book is a beautifully designed thing with exquisitely moulded letters as headers – the work of Ross's brother (in the audience along with Mrs Ross and their three kids). The little ones didn't seem to mind Ross's sometimes robust language.

Pip Griffin read a selection from her several poetry books and in interview talked about her time in choirs and writing theatre pieces with cohort Penelope Grace.

In the second half, Paul Knoebel presented a response to the Sydney Biennale, which festival Penelope commented on. 'I saw a lot of things I didn't expect and I didn't have the faintest idea what it meant but at least it was free admission.'

August Live Poets was billed in the local paper as a Mexican fiesta. Mario Cabrera came to read his poems and Diego Espejel played guitar and sang Spanish songs from heartfelt ballads and lullabies to the odd ode to the lewd ('Cockaracha!').

There was a chilli con carne with beans instead of beef supper prepared by this convenor. Mariarchi music and bullfight troubadours serenaded patrons as they entered the sitting room. I attempted to interview Mario but he literally kept wandering off in a trance – grinning around a door jamb a moment later –

preferring to answer any questions in his poems amid his voice's haunting timbre. He was there to promote his book *Yuxtas* (*back and forth*), but I wanted to discuss too his translations of Australian poets for South Americans and his background as a puppeteer in his old country.

As regards Mario and Diego's interaction, generally Mario would start with a brace of poems then at intervals he would wander away and Diego would do a bracket before Mario drifted back anew. It was Cabaret Latina, the rousing often bawdy songs a nice foil for Mario's more sombre aching phrases – the last stanzas emphasising how life always has a trick up its sleeve so best not to worry, just play it out, like a Borges, like a Cervantes.

In the courtyard, Bill had us hang up a huge banner for climate change (courtesy of his Parramatta action group) and people crowded round to get in the picture.

In September, John Tranter was at Don Bank to commemorate forty years since the Generation of 68 – and the Schism that has gone down in poetry lore in this country when the Establishment was challenged then superseded by the New Breed armed with Xerox copiers and ideas of protest in the shadow of the Vietnam War.

The whole business of getting published was being turned on its head, as Tranter explained. Echoes of Pop turning the art world over to the people. A revolution poetry was ready for, if no one else was. Yet to the outside world these poetry wars were like the threat of members of the Poets Union later to withdraw their labour because of this and that outrage – subsumed in a game of egos.

Poetry being the most subjective art is always susceptible to that. It all ultimately depended on who could secure the seat of influence. In reality, 1968 was not really about storming the citadel of power. It was about taking poetry out of the citadel forever. The genie was free of the bottle and now anything could happen. Tranter stressed he was reporting the action rather than pushing the buttons but appreciated change was in the air anyway and the 'free' voices had no choice but to prove they were better, more effective.

It certainly stopped a lot of kowtowing and imaginary dressing of professors without portfolios or some such. If there were more opportunities for real poets of skill, who could complain? The end result now I suppose is everybody creating their own event on Facebook.

Anyhow there was the Shake-Up and the Re-Alignment. The pizzazz around those happenings was well expressed by John's illo for the PR leaflet with the breathless description 'Young writers had decided drugs and sex were not enough. They wanted more! Much more!'

Meantime, Paul Buckberry did a song or two and there was a healthy number of regulars keen to hear about 1968 and continue with their business of communicating in 2008.

October was time for some African Incantations. Dorothy Makasa from Zambia was a poet I'd met through performing with Auburn Poets and Writers at the Sydney Writers Festival in May. I had been entranced by the musical vowels of her Bemba dialect then. During our interview, she talked about the *griots*, the local soothsayers and shamans employed to sing the praises of religious figures and politicians; to give thanks and blessings to the happy couple at weddings, and so on. I was familiar with *griots* performing a more independent role in Mali. We also talked about the conundrum of the West's relationship with Africa: doing harm when wanting to do such good. Dorothy called her poems incantations. Their rhythmic power captivated attention.

To stanchion the African vibe, I had the favourite stories of Nelson Mandela read to the audience and served up Cabbage

Zulu, an African dish, at supper. African music on the stereo greeted patrons as they entered.

In the open section, Paul Knoebel read a poem from *Blast!*, an English literary magazine of the 1930s founded by the Imagists. Peter Wagner read a poem to his friend Les Murray (on Les's 70th birthday) and told of helping save Bunyah (the Murray homestead near Buhladelah, NSW) from a fire that broke out while Peter was visiting Les. Bill Tibben read about photographs being forbidden at an Albert Namitjira + Utes Exo at Hermannsburg Mission, NT. And there were two beautiful pieces from Cathy Bray (first time at Don Bank and I spelt her name with a K!). The poems just glistened up at you like jewels – just so – and then were gone. At the end of the night we danced around to the music of Hugh Masakela.

In November, because we were featuring performance poet Miles Merrill, I decided to institute some seating changes at Don Bank. I arranged the chairs not in their usual straight lines up and down but forming a circle, with the poets reading from the middle surrounded by the audience. In the event, Miles was late arriving and hobbling sheepishly when he got there. There'd been a mishap at a gig the night before and he'd injured his leg! He would be doing all his vaunted performing from the sitting position.

Helen was also late arriving with the supper and there was a patch-on-the-run twist to the program. Peter Wagner asked some pertinent questions when he opened the batting. 'What if the poets didn't turn up? What if the audience didn't show?' 'What if the poems did not arrive?' 'What if the poems came but no one else?' To which Lee Cass's self-amped slide guitar was a mettlesome foil. Stephen Jurd hit the spot with his poem 'about Warnie'.

Then it was Miles. Merrill comes from Chicago and was asked why he came to Oz? How was it going to schools and colleges talking to students about the poetry performance craft? What is it inside a person that compels them to be a character in front of an audience? He then proceeded to give a stirring, word-curdling demo of his art.

In the second half, Jenny Lee, who won the A Cappella Song Contest the last time Don Bank held one, took us through several classics on the piano including a love poem to Caledonia and a Joni Mitchell Xmas; also a song based on a Shafic Ataya poem which positively ached. I remember talking to a very ill and down Shafic that morning on the phone.

Maureen Ten invited this convenor to do a two-hander mini-play. Bob Howe's poets ended up banished to the yellow pages after being too serious. Suzie Rourke made us laugh with the role of 'LOL's in SMS texts. The UnDarwin Awards were announced.

Scatter Pattern

It burns a hole
Of numbness in the very mind you use
To hold them safe, to know that those you love
Will be erased from time without a trace.
Of course, you muse,
Clutching whatever fancy may console
Foretasted grief, it's true
That all of history's monsters have to face
Annihilation too,
With all the horrors they were guilty of.

Each cell, they say,
Of tissue, every earthly speck was sent,
And ultimately dust of some dead star,
Intergalactic scatterings which earn us
Embodiment.
There in the glove box of your car today
An atom lies, once flung
From out of a supernova's bursting furnace,
Or fastens on your tongue,
Exchanged in one French kiss, from just as far.

Maybe some flecks
Of mind, no less than matter, do survive,
Some psychic smatterings of fear and danger
Flung from the murderous will of Tamerlane,
And still alive
In your most idle musings. And effects,
The merest motes of grace
Of one it numbs your heart to lose, remain,
In you, yes, but their trace
Dispersed to some unborn and distant stranger.

Stephen Edgar

Shells

in memory of Andrew McNaughtan, 1953–2003

Over the harbour coves today
the air feels thinner.

On the sand near Castle Rock
I pick up a faded purple shell,
its outer ridges gnarled
as an old boxer's knuckles,
the inner surface
smooth as a sigh.

I'd put a note on his door,
'Call me urgently',
but the house already felt like a shell.
He had no children
but the children of Timor.

It hadn't rained for weeks
then, at the funeral,
torrents burst.

It won't feel the same
going down to the bay.

I rub my finger over the shell,
comforting as Andrew's smile
even when our despair
was deep as the harbour.

Brendan Doyle

Cross-examination – a Walk on the Wild Side

Head for the top of William Street –
pause, for a moment, to admire the giant Coca-Cola sign – drink it in!
And take in the famous 'dog balls on sticks' sculpture.
Then, turn sharp left, into Darlinghurst Road.
Head towards McDonalds and the big round fountain.
This 'patch' is the least salubrious in area code 2011.

Some of its features have never changed: prostitutes –
and their pimps, druggies, dance girls and their spruikers,
short of talent and clothing, but prepared
to prance, near-nude, on minute stages.
Police, ever-present, sometimes in twos and threes but all sexes and sizes
others on radio call as required. Once as rough as needed, to maintain control,
their touch is gentler now – with community policing.

Most striking, is what I call the 'eyeball syndrome'.
Spotted, throughout the area are drinking holes and bars.
At all hours they can be crowded, many middle-aged
and older men front available spaces, the bars often
open to the air at the front, to allow smoking. The
drinkers scan all passers-by, not least the women, not
always unpleasantly. The gaze often seems indifferent
if not well meant, as its owner is often half-sozzled.
Their eyes are bloodshot, jaundiced, dazed and vague.
We passers-by, try to avoid their looks, or
return them subtly and not too prominently. The
overall impression is one of discomfort and not pleasure.
A morbid, decadent spirit prevails – reminiscent of the 'old' Cross,
– violent and possibly dangerous.
We are glad there is glass between us, as we pass.

We do not look back, as if, like Eurydice, we might also
turn to stone – by those already stoned.
Each day, I walk this way, on my way, to the local station –
it's a test I've always passed – in my cross-examination.

Peter Wagner

Sunday Sailor

And suddenly the dusky shearwaters are gone
leaving none abaft and none abeam;
neither glancing off the shore-bound crests astern
and chasing down the *Pea-pod*'s transom,
for a flitting daytime ghost beside:

there's no grey breast to port or starboard
not one fleet speck on greys of sea and cloud
but all are taken up in a fingerlight of sun
like a rainbow's end, never here but just beyond.

Look! A mile seaward they gyre and swoop
now wide, now close like cyclone-scraps
flung down but tight-leashed to some god's hand.
To gravity of birth? To frenzy of blood?
I sail out to look.

Pea-pod butts against a whale-browed billow.
Sea-teeth block cloud-light and swallow
the wide laughing waters down a blue-black gullet.
I stand, lift arms and supplicate.
'Not *Sea-quad* but *Pea-pod*'

I show empty palms, and plead,
'Just a mousy, moulting urban chap
not a white and desperate harpooneer.'
and I ooch the yellow-bellied dinghy
around the maw of the sea.

The wind is a white cat stretched out across the sky,
lazing in the sun, twitching silver whiskers.
He reaches down a paw,
ruffles water and pats the sail
with velveted, smirking claw.

Slender, travellers' wings sling round the masthead.
Under their circle, folded wings paddle.
Underwater, the birds fly after silver-bellies
and shed bubbles from iridescent plumage
then bob up; swallow, shake and start; take fright.

Earth rolls the flock under Cat-in-the-sky;
my sail backs and flaps in veering wind.
A fresh sea-breeze leans on the flinching spar.
Pea-pod spins about, surfs and rolls to shelter
chased by cat-claws flashing on a choppy sea.

Henry Sheerwater

Happy Endings

It takes four of us, on foot, to scare
the cows in from the agistment paddocks, and even when
they cluster in a green chasm beside water
the neighbour's useless mongrel bolts yapping
through the middle of the herd. You've got to pelt
rocks at him, run blaspheming after the strays

till they blunder into the stockyard then bellow
backwards away from the truck ramp before
the cattle prod's rump-jolting singe
tilts the equation of terror. One of them shits
a green dollop into your boot, khaki urine
cascades over the truck's iron decking, bowels and bladders

blossom in adrenaline chaos. Not one of us knows how
to tell them this is a day for happy endings –
not every cattle truck skulks to the death house and
today's final solution is their home pasture
furred with rye-grass for the milk already glimmering
in the great gut where their work makes them free.

Craig Powell

Atget's Paris 1898–1927

Ghost images in sepia
lie trapped in a photographer's old plates
within *boulangerie* and *boucherie*
on boulevard, Pont-Neuf, the Seine

fortifications zone shanties
ragged, boned and disarrayed
survive a dank, dilapidated outer-world
rank, redolent of desperation and despair

contorted roofs and monumental buildings
shove, jostle, elbow in picturesque déshabillé
while narrow cobbled back lanes
squeeze emptiness until it hurts

melancholy corners of old gardens
hide stone steps that moulder into deep decay
an alabaster figure mimes *grande guignol*
against the Tuileries' shocked trees

Montmartre, Moulin de la Gallette
are people-less, *sans* sleaze *sans* smell
a petrified gargoyle shrieks silently
on some Parisienne's decrepit tomb.

Pip Griffin

After an exhibition of the historic photographs of Eugène Atget at the Art Gallery of New South Wales, September 2012.

The New Cooking

Ready, Steady, Fornicate.
Can't Fornicate, Won't Fornicate.
Fornicating with Nigella.
Fornicating, not wishing to discriminate, with Rhodes.
The F word.
Ramsay's Bedroom Nightmares.
The Galloping Gourmet
Fornicator.
Fornicate with Fanny,
although not in colour.
Two Fat Ladies (on a motorbike)
Fornicating.
School Dinners with…no,
maybe not.
French Fornicating Made Simple.
The Ten Minute Fornicator.
Fornicating for Beginners.
Fornicating for Health.
Fornicating for Life.
The Organic Fornicator.
Vegetarian Fornicating at Home.
You Are What You Fornicate.
And, for the young leaving home
in these straitened times,
Fornicating for Flatters and
Fornicating on a Budget.
Fornicating – a hobby for life.
The new cooking.

Ross Hattaway

Vicky Viidikas in 1974

for Robert Adamson

I'm looking at you 24 years
before you passed away

I gaze and gaze at you and I guess
we could have been very good friends.

And maybe shifted beyond, one never
knows where or when a friendship

ends. And I'm talking to you in this
way not just because of your addictions:

alcohol, sex, drugs…but far more than that:
your smile your face – indeed, a poem in itself…

Mario Licón-Cabrera

My Sister

My sister feels sexy today, she says. I think
she just feels needy as usual. Those guys
on the porch, tell them to piss off. Why?
Because if you feel needy, who needs you?
Needy is like greedy, let's not pretend
it's just a rhyme like 'got' and 'hot'. You
know rhymes exist for a reason, like lying
down after lunch in the heat or lying to them
about what you said you did last night: you're not
so hot, Honey. South of the Border you might be
a pole dancer or some señorita in need, but
not here, understand? Go then to Mexico, be
honest, say what you really mean to them,
those men on the porch, be sweet and be
yourself, be a thing-in-itself itself, and I'll be a
thing-for-you in case you need Some Thing
other than my regard, the thing you can't really
ask for, the thing you hate about the heat, that you
can't turn off, South of the Border it's hot.

John Tranter

'My Sister' began as a draft using the end-words of 'Soft Money' by
Rae Armantrout, from *The Best of the Best American Poetry* page 23.

Ubuntu e chalo – Our Humanity a Universe

Ibula te chimuti,
Ichimitii e mpanga,
impanga e chalo.

A leaf is not a tree.
The tree is a forest,
the forest is a universe.

Umubili te muntu,
umuntu e bantu,
abantu e buntu,
ubuntu e chalo.

A body is not a person,
the person is human,
humans are humanity,
humanity is a universe.

Ishina lyandi tefyo ndi,
naba mu chimo chandi,
Ichimo chandi e chalo.

My name is not I am,
I am is my presence,
my presence is a universe.

Dorothy Makasa

Truculence (Teen Valkyrie)

Truculence storms out slamming the door
in high dudgeon.
Absolutely enraged, apropos of nothing
other than we are staying and she is out of here.

The anger of the middle child
which we can't understand…

> I was the youngest in the most adored
> and privileged of positions.
> You, the oldest, using and abusing
> the power that entailed…

And here our middling child
stuck between two bookends.

Every day an Icelandic crusade.
Our teen Valkyrie puts her horns on,
Her backpack leaves her sword-hand free.
The 433 deposits her on the distant shore.

She strides the sandhills scowling
and scans the far horizon.
A wave of relief washes over her
– all her friends are there.

Waiting for her, near The Valhalla.

Cathy Bray

Performed by Cathy Bray at her 2012 Sydney Fringe show *Inappropriate.*

Flickatharist

In olden times to stay your station
In typical self-deprecation
Our Aussie spin was heard to twist
All daring skills – 'A flick o' the wrist'

An ageing sportsman with a ball
Would seem no barrier at all
But many batters' hearts he's torn
Because to this art he was born

Oh many papers he has sold
And all the tawdry tales were told
But batters feel their fate forlorn
Whenever they must face Shane Warne

Stephen Jurd

Poetry and Presenting it in Public
Part Two

Why do you go to hear other people read/perform?

David Falcon: Just as for every exhibition of paintings I see or every musical concert I listen to, there are only one or two pieces that stand out – so it is for me with poetry. But when in that sense a poem does really stand out it makes the whole endeavour of listening and writing poetry worth the effort.

Benito di Fonzo: Because good poets borrow, but great poets steal. I wrote that. Seriously, it can be a beautiful moment to hear someone come out with something you wish you had written. And if they don't, then that can just encourage you.

Richard James Allen: The poems lift off the page. I like to hear poets' voices, distinguishing one matrix of mind, body, emotion, language and history from another, or hearing similarities or shared lineages. Though it has to be said that poets are sometimes the worst actual performers of their poems. For that reason, I also like to hear other people besides the authors present their work – they often bring fresh perspectives to the text and an aliveness to the delivery of the language.

Susan Adams: I do it to learn.

Kate Lilley: I hear the work differently and enjoy the embodied experience.

Ernest Zehentner: Maybe a way of checking what is happening… maybe a nasty streak to see people embarrass themselves…maybe the same reason an artist goes to a gallery. Notice how kids sit in a circle when one of them gets up and does a nursery rhyme.

Bill Tibben: I go so that I earn my turn – because poetry is interesting, fundamental, as a form of human communication.

Cathy Bray: I go to see what they have to say and why they had to write a poem to do it.

Les Wicks: To be enriched and to be supportive of the reader/performer.

Scott Sandwich: It's really, really fun. Or at least it should be.

Edwin Wilson: Of later years, because of my increasing deafness, I have tended to avoid most social functions that require aural skills. These days, I find it incredibly hard to hear what people are saying when there is background noise of any kind, and mentally exhausting as I try to cobble together an amalgam of conversations from lip-reading and body language, cadence and syllables, and the occasional heard word.

What triggers the biggest buzz when reading/performing for you?

Richard James Allen: When you feel you have really hit the mark, perfectly delivered a particular poem to a particular audience at a particular time and place. You have often [in so doing] discovered something you didn't know about your work and your abilities, even if you had previously planned and rehearsed your presentation. Therefore you feel truly alive in the moment exploring your potential as a writer and a performer, living your art.

Erwin Zehentner: Standing up in front of a crowd and seeing two or twenty pairs of eyes looking at you expectantly.

David Falcon: The biggest buzz for me is hearing a piece that really touches me. This not only gives me a buzz at the time but leaves me with something to carry forward.

Scott Sandwich: Performing is a buzz! I try really hard not to make it Myself versus the Audience, though. I make sure my work is conversational, and real and natural. The biggest buzz is when you see an audience realise they're not being talked at.

It's the same way the biggest buzz in a friendship is when you click with the other person – that moment when you realise that something you've just said has made you better friends. If it's a heartbreaking line for you, you can feel an audience feel it too, and you know this audience is worth giving more energy to. If they laugh when you want them to, or even at an unexpected moment, you think, 'I like this crowd! I'm going to give them everything.'

Benito di Fonzo: Getting a good reaction from the audience. Particularly if it's a good reaction! Although a bad is better than nothing I suppose…

Kate Lilley: The sense that the work makes an impact, produces a response.

Les Wicks: I would say, the unexpected.

Philip Radmall: Audience appreciation. And being in the presence of people who want to listen to you – it sort of validates the effort and the work itself sometimes.

Candy Royalle: Knowing my audience is there with me, on the journey.

Martin Langford: Quality meanings perfectly inflected into the emotional space.

Paul Buckberry: I am a performer and crave the interaction. That said, some of my most memorable moments in life have come through reading a poem [to myself] and acknowledging the illumination.

Cathy Bray: When I realise by the audience reaction that they have understood what I'm trying to say – by laughter, by groans, by smiles, by frowns, by gasps.

Willem Tibben: By getting a deep response when I'm reading/performing. Sensing I have made a connection. Knowing for myself that I did a good one. Sometimes an interaction with the audience as part of the presenting is a buzz. Sometimes the tense silence of deep listening. Being affected/touched/moved by hearing a poem that 'hits' me.

Edwin Wilson: One of the biggest buzzes I ever had was at the launch of *Cosmos Seven* (Woodbine Press, 1998) at Live Poets at Don Bank. A lot of my long-suffering friends had come along that night, and this was the last time I invited most of them to book launches, as I was becoming embarrassed by the increasing frequency of such events – that they should feel obligated to buy another book. Shirley Colless, Deputy Lord Mayor of North Sydney – whom I had worked with on a book and exhibition project at the Royal Botanic Gardens where I worked – said a few kind words. Somehow we got onto my poem 'Ancient Bouquet', which I had had translated into hieroglyphs! Then Sue and Danny and a number of my friends contributed to what became a memorable night.

Are poetry competitions over-rated?

Willem Tibben: Quite possibly. I am ambivalent about this, having won very few – think of a number bigger than zero and smaller than two…

Kate Lilley: Yes, though useful in various ways. The terms of entry and the choice of judges set the outcome.

Martin Langford: Hugely. They mean a little, but not much.

Paul Buckberry: Yes. Art is not sport, it's not a competition.

Les Wicks: Overrated? Yes and no.

Susan Adams: Yes, I think so. With this age of digital communication, the number of international poems received is too many to be assessed [properly].

Erwin Zehentner: An interesting concept. As I discovered when researching racing cars, as soon as two cars appeared on a road, they had to prove to themselves which one was quicker than the other. Throughout civilisation there's always been competition between people – why should poetry or art be exempt? How you judge this is another matter. A poem/artwork can be absolutely awful but if it satisfies technical parameters it may well win. It often comes down to beauty being in the eye of the beholder - and the background of the judges.

Scott Sandwich: I'm not sure I'd say competitions and slams are over-rated…I just think they play a different role for an audience than they should for the performers. For a poet, I think a poetry competition is a great place to practise, develop skills, and try things. I want to be writing and performing poetry for its own sake, the same way I would if I were writing music, or putting on theatre. I just want to make art, a thing that stands by itself. If I write with the intention of trying to win, or to 'better' someone else, I often find myself writing dishonestly… I have faith that audiences aren't stupid enough to fall for it, that they know when I'm trying to impress them rather than sharing something or inviting them in. Besides, in the long run, those poems inevitably suck. On top of that, when you're at a slam where winning doesn't matter, then you should be able to perform anything. I suppose my answer is that poetry competitions are over-rated when the emphasis is on the competition…but we all know that, don't we?

David Falcon: I don't take too much notice of poetry competitions, although I will often read the winning poems to see what it is that people like. I think the most useful function of competitions is to allow poets to establish a reputation.

Richard James Allen: Poetry competitions can be useful as part of the business of poetry – deadlines to work towards, opportunities to build the poet's CV and sense of existing in the world. They also generate media – or at least, social media – buzz, creating the momentum around an event. I have judged a number of poetry competitions and they certainly have their place in drawing a poetry community together and facilitating the emergence of new voices. But I think that as a form they can become a little tedious. Ultimately, in my opinion, poetry is about the spirit, which connects us all, not competition between our small selves, which divides us. Poetry competitions can provide energy, excitement and focus, and they have their own inherent drama, but I don't feel that poetry needs to become a sport to be interesting.

Phil Radmall: Over-rated? Not if you win!

Candy Royalle: I think that poetry competitions might offer people some recognition that they crave. Personally, I'm indifferent. I think they are what they are – people can choose to engage or not.

Benito di Fonzo: Poetry should not be competitive. It's not a sport, it's not a business. However, these days people have been socialised that they should only back the 'winner' or 'victor'. It's part of the post-industrial culture of entrepreneurial violence that is our happy age. So if it takes competitions to get venues and audiences on board, so be it.

Edwin Wilson: All poetry competitions, prizes and literary grants, because of their nature, must be highly subjective – and prone to be 'political' as well, I would suspect.

Cathy Bray: Worse than over-rated, poetry competitions are damaging to the art of poetry. I write because I have something to say and no other way to say it – not by a novel, not by a play, not by an advertisement. I can't fulfil that brief by jumping over false hurdles with false reasons for writing via imposed rules and competitions, themed anthologies, topical poems, and so on.

LIVE POETS AT
DON BANK

FOURTH WEDNESDAY OF EVERY MONTH (FEBRUARY-NOVEMBER)

6 NAPIER STREET, NORTH SYDNEY

$7 Admission includes supper and liquid refreshment
7.30 – 10.30 pm

INQUIRIES: 9896 6956 dannylivepoets@yahoo.com.au

All welcome to recite, sing, tell a story, play
an instrument or just listen if you'd like to!

WEDNESDAY
SEPTEMBER 23rd

GIANT OPEN SECTION

POEMS/SONGS ABOUT SPACE

POEMS/SONGS ABOUT
. . .
THE FUTURE

Hear rock-stars reaching for the heavens
with Special Guest: WAYNE GILLESPIE.

Drawing by an Ashaday (South American Indian) boy

2009

We had a special guest from the UK, Claire Naylor, to kick off the season and a young local poet on the rise in Jacob Ziguras.

Claire was a performance poet from Liverpool's Merseyside on her Dead Good Down Under Tour, a past winner of the Liverpool Slam and runner up in the Monsters of Poetry in Belfast. She was witty, frank, endearing. She joked about her mother, who was scared of Claire going to the Cavern in Liverpool to see 'those Beatles'. Claire didn't do an out and out performance *sans* script but her between-poems patter was top shelf. She would make a good host of a live show.

Jacob Ziguras by contrast in the second half didn't take himself seriously enough to reward an interview. Jacob's poetry is beautiful, powerful, lyrical. It seems he has still to find his big subject and identity. He tends towards the anthropomorphic – like the younger Ted Hughes. How the maturing of the colder, philosopher's eye changes his focus will be interesting to watch.

In the open section, Cathy Bray again showed an adroit use of words and a honed technique. Ron Wilkins softened his more solemn edges with traces of wit. Lee Cass broke up all the words with his rolling slide guitar – and he had a book of anecdotes about Bondi to sell. He knows how to charm a crowd. Big Marty has been coming to Live Poets for some time but not reading. This night he professed to being bipolar. There was a definite edge about him and he exploited that when he decided to read. I had the weirdest feeling after his first poem's bitter recognition of inadequacy that he now had the gun pulled on us and society was about to pay. Did I tell you? It's February again.

The special guests in March were both locals – John Carey from Chatswood, who was presenting his new book, and Jacques Goldman.

John is a practised performer and took us through a range of subject matter and character types. He leans towards the cynical, but the wryness hits home before that. There are few prisoners or dubious heroes in JC's world; there is the scalpel of his observation, there is much ridiculousness we celebrate.

Goldman spoke mainly in aphorisms. The inferences were slow to take up at times. He often inhabits the mind of the child – pathos is a byword. Any interview of Jacques would only get in the way. He would prefer to interview our emotions and we would see what he found there.

It was a small gathering this night but there were some gems from the regulars. David Wansbrough told an anecdote re a bipolar woman who said, 'Meet me in the Blue Mountains @ 9.37 tomorrow (Sunday) morning.' Another memorable couplet from his second piece was 'so you're a poor poet from Moscow, you're too fat to be a poet' – this from the mouth of a courtesan at a party.

In April, Kate Maclurcan was back – on a night that would present poems and songs about/from childhood.

The open section was interspersed with anecdotes from famous childhoods; quotes from personalities such as Mary Gilmore, Bill O'Reilly, Thomas Keneally, Kenneth Slessor, Michael Leunig, Annette Shun Wah, Aiden Ridgeway and Peter Sculthorpe. There were readings from the book, *Poems of Guantanamo*, with its inevitable echoes to Live Poets Press' *Open Boat – Barbed Wire Sky*.

The room was close to full. Kate's set was the usual high quality of her own material with beckings to folk heroes Leonard Cohen and Bernard Bolan, who she always interprets so individually.

The open section was in rare form: Maurice Whelan presented an evocative piece about his father. Suzie Rourke a story about her horse 'Thunder'. Bob Howe presented the Poetry

Poet which ended, 'How am I not a poet? I write a poem which is not about oranges and called it – Oranges' (ref Frank O' Hara).

After supper, David Falcon told about 'Dad's Breakfast'. Lee Cass slid his way to WA to find his father. After Sue Hicks' 'Song for a Six Year Old', the crowd laughed, loved and felt sorry for Humpty Dumpty. After the Guantanamo poems, Jenny Campbell presented 'The News' in a cabaret style, a stark New Depression world. She's more humorous and has better structures now – still with the same searing observations. She put it down to her attending the Comedy Store lately and 'imbibing' stand-up.

What is Weird Poetry? Verse that deals with the paranormal? This was the question posed by the local paper in its preview of the guest appearance of Leigh Blackmore at Don Bank – who would do a reading from and discuss that very topic with his publisher – Lane Cove's Danny Lockhart (P'rea Press).

Leigh was not as scary as we expected. He does convene a covenant in Wollongong (but what do they do at their meetings was not explained). He tried to find a cheery poem to start and succeeded with light irony. The crowd kept applauding. 'Poetry is not that popular and weird poetry is a small part of that,' he lent perspective.

Danny L came up to talk about the structure, execution and heritage of weird poetry. 'It goes where other forms do not. A lot of it drawn from the past.' 'You mean Gothic?' someone interjected. The audience now joined the discussion, led by Peter Wagner and Bob Howe in the main. They posited, 'It seems to be a deathless element speaking to the child's nightmare in the adult mind.' People agreed that you could see this went back to before poetry was written down. In an ancient Sumerian myth told by a woman, someone offered. In Australia, the natives told stories around the corroborree fire and theatre informed the song cycles and so on.

Danny L moved on to discussion about his new publishing press and what projects were planned for the future.

There was something of a 'Gong invasion of the open section, with supporters of Leigh and weird poetry. Margaret Curtis started it off, followed by Andreas Crowthorne. 'Perry' did some ditties by Raymond Chandler. Maurice Whelan's poem shimmered with intent. Donna's story wandered into a flabby denouement. David Falcon teased us with an adaptation of 'You all know the Next Line' from Edgar Allan Poe. Kyla was nothing less than witchy. She knew the value of the pause – teasing last night's dream into our daylight. It was transfixing and signalled a warning.

June led to a somewhat weird situation, with Lee offering to introduce me beginning a reading of this convenor's new book *Before I Press the Trigger* and then me expecting to be asked about the background to some of the poems. I was waiting for Lee to interview me and I had written down the questions for him! It was not the best situation for a convenor to put himself in!

Jenny Campbell, the other guest that night, did a witty, charming, continually evolving interview and she and this convenor were relaxation itself. Jenny then brought out the hits: 'Water', 'Butterflies' and 'Class' (an hilarious polarising of opposites). Saddam's execution in 'Barbaric Grist' brought blunt facts and repercussions to the fore.

Bill Tibben's tale of the cow continued from last month and included this line: 'a dirigible deflated – she'll live'.

July was a concept night. Voices From Asia – Sherry Chan (China) Sri Bhagavadas (Sri Lanka) and Dona Zappone (Malaysia) – with the added delight of a late-evening Fadeel Kayat from Iraq.

The open section was asked to offer poems or music from their travels in Asia. Only Rosemary Huisman followed this directive, with a short resonant piece on a visit to India. Richard

Jenner from Auburn Poets and Writers Group came to support Dona and Sri. A copy of their anthology, *Auburn Letters*, was raffled along with Sherry Chan's *Moonlight of Romance*. The three guests regaled in their interviews with how they found Australia.

Sri worked for the Redfern Legal Service and told how he was mistaken by people in outback NSW for being Aboriginal. Sherry related the story of how she put her poems, written while recovering from illness, in the window of her Surry Hills unit and this ended up attracting the attention of Live Poets regulars Penelope Grace and Pip Griffin, who promptly invited her to a poetry reading. Dona's childhood was a time of ghosts and Chinese temples – painting pictures in her mind. She would develop into an artist as well as a writer. Fadeel coming later somewhat alchemically transposed the rhythms of his native Iraq into English. The images seemed inevitable but continually becoming – falling miraculously into confirmation. There was also a teasing story of a trip to Norway when Fadeel went out of his way to attend to a woman bogged down in a Skype problem. In his recent project researching the re-establishment of the Marsh Arabs in Iraq post-Saddam Hussein, Fadeel sought to revive the words and deeds of populations thought disappeared. He came back with agents of his rescue mission – flutes made in the old way from the vegetation of a recovered region.

This convenor had been impressed by Emily Ballou's event at the recent Sydney Writers Festival. Emily's book about the life of Charles Darwin (who died in 1909) was made up of poems about various stages in the great naturalist's career. In these poems, Emily invoked the characters of various people in Darwin's life in vivid re-enactments. I thought she would be an absorbing guest at Don Bank in August. The consequent interview sought to get behind the making of the *Darwin Poems*, from concept into being. Emily obliged by re-plotting her research in England. She also touched upon Darwin's time in Australia – his seminal walks in the Blue Mountain that now bear trails in his name. She was keen to stress that her poems weren't seeking to remake history. She was not putting herself in the person of Darwin as he did this and that. Every incident in her book had its research source reference. The poetry did help the reader make the essential imaginative leap, however.

September's Live Poets sought to honour the UN Year of Astronomy, with Poems and Songs about Space/the Future.

In the open section, poets were asked to present material on this theme. A special guest to help out on the songs was guitarist Wayne Gillespie, who had previously featured at Don Bank. In a night (hopefully) of illumination and innovation befitting the Wide Frontier, there would be a re-enactment of the Apollo landing of 1969 fulfilling John Kennedy's dream of putting a man on the moon.

The evening was kicked off with some Aboriginal legends, including that of the Seven Sisters; their escape from a wilful master plotted in stars in the Milky Way of the outback sky. Suzie Rourke's poem then asked, 'What did I see in the Night?'

There was a poem about Pluto from Nur Alam of APWG read by this convenor. Danny Lockhart contributed 'Red Man Moving'. There was Kevin Hart's poem about the future. Janet Reynolds read Craig Raine's 'EarthWise'. Bill Tibben and this convenor were then seated at the controls of the Houston space centre and the Apollo 9 module respectively while Cathy Bray provided beeps monitoring the transcript of communication between the two on her mobile phone.

This was real life, installation and sound sculpture all rolled into one, the participants praying the suspension of disbelief held as the lunar module hovered over its target!

Just before the supper break, the room was plunged into

darkness and then a sequence called 'Astronauts Anonymous' erupted. This convenor illuminated his face with torchlight to successive testimonies from NASA's foot soldiers in space. One particularly memorable quote included was that of Buzz Aldrin: 'We were too solemn about what we did up there [on the moon] on film. We should have goofed around more!'

After the supper break, Wayne Gillespie came on to do some songs – 'Skin', 'Geriatric Blues', 'Satellite of Love (with this convenor on vocal in Lou Reed dark glasses), 'Starman' (Danny on vocal), 'Rocket Man' (with Suzie Rourke and boyfriend Glenn on vocals). Danny Lockhart's limerick ad Review and Bruce Dawe's 'Time Capsule' and Suzie's poem to her brother completed the open section. There were numerous quotes about the future to finish what had been a night out of the ordinary people decided.

Maurice Whelan, with his book *The Lilac Bow*, was the guest for October. There was an informative interview about his life and work. The reading was sublime and professional – honed, Maurice assured me, by his relentless spruiking of his writing at numerous events and guest spots in NSW and the rest of the eastern seaboard.

After the inspiration of those crafted but urgent poems, Gilmar and Juan made the place erupt with a sublime interplay – Spanish guitar playing on bass and lead. It was the complementary ingredient of music after words that Don Bank loves. There should have been far more people to watch it and this convenor decided he'd erred in not having the music first – or perhaps bracketing Maurice's interview and set.

It remained for two of Australia's finest poets – Louise Wakeling and Martin Harrison – to see out the year. The PR leaflet for this night was designed like a classic Australian movie poster featuring 'Paragliding Bees' (incorporating the poets' latest titles: 'Paragliding in a War Zone' and 'Wild Bees') starring Louise and Martin. This involved lively interviews with the poets and generous readings.

Louise prompted some laughs with tales of her assignment to visit and teach poetry to inmates in Silverwater prison. To quote one example, 'Yeah, I've got a hacksaw in this cake!' Louise opined to nervous guards – the cake concerned cooked by her for a prisoner's birthday. She wondered also how a visit to the correctional while pregnant might have informed the sensibilities of her future son.

Martin had us in stitches recounting his time at Yaddo – a writers' retreat in New York state – and shocked us by voicing an unresolved ambition to compose poetry out of sounds rather than speech. Had that been inspired by David Byrnes 'found' sounds in Arab Africa being turned into music (à la Music from the Bush of Ghosts)?

Louise's work mark her as arguably Australia's premier female poet and Martin's effortless touch and mesmerising tone magnified the everyday. OK, it was hard to stop his irrepressible raconteuring bent. It was hard too for the open section to compete with how those two had taken us to the movies. There is this jotted quote while someone was reading – this convenor just can't recall who was responsible for the lines. 'Time moves too fast for us to live again. I wait for the girl who said, "Wait here – I will remember you. Wait here." And so finally when I am remade I can move on.' The song ends with him, this poet? calling out to the forest, hoping to emulate, emanate her. 'Did I hear him or her, a fly, sharpened by my hunger?' The question echoes.

The Right Fundamentals

I knew his eyes immediately.
A fire burned
not brightly –
but fiercely.

It's hardly possible to slink
behind your essence.
It takes a great deal of training
to be such an illusionist
and he was not.
He was clumsy, as transparent as a patriot's pride.

He talked of 'evil'.

'There's no such thing!'
I countered,
'Evil is the shroud of your clandestine contortions,
used to connote every social tragedy
every act of desperation
every move to sovereign defence.'

He looked at me as though he could squash me like a dangerous bug.

He went on to damn the most visionary scientists
to a hellish world of his conception.
They wanted to transform disease
into the servant of man.
He believed disease was man's
punishment:

'The world is overpopulated,' he said.

He applauded the downfall of those whose
Hippocratic Oath helped women's wombs
be free of unwanted occupancy,
arguing the minutest of cells capable of building houses.

Moral trespassing was a pastime he pursued in broad daylight.

He never saw the sun rise
without believing today was the day
that man would pay.

The horsemen of the Apocalypse
would be his saviours
and if possible
he would be riding them,
ripping into beauty and passion

with poisoned spurs
and jagged whips,
building an eternal firestorm
to pitch all sinners and their
evil hearts into the arms of Lucifer.

He dreamt of bygone days
of public torture
universal death sentiment
the erasure of the love that dare not speak its name
and those godless atheists.

He positively salivated at the idea of a new McCarthy.
He even imagined it might be himself
penning the name of his opponents
and calling them in to answer for their crimes
against his ethos.

His fantasies spiralled dangerously toward the ownership of
all the fruits of man's march through time
righteously believing them to be rightfully his
to use or discard.
The blaze of his winter hearth would be fuelled
by the under-utilised books of great philosophy.

Yes, I knew him,
but he didn't scare me
he disgusted me.

His attire was not the hijab
and he had never had cause to smoke a strawberry sheesha pipe
or write from right to left.
He wore jeans and a nike T-shirt
and he called himself a good Christian.

He said he possessed
the right fundamentals.
'Close,' I was compelled to say, 'you have
the fundamentals of the right.'

Unbelievably, I had met a grotesque carbon copy
of a frightful phenomenon that had reached
its zenith once before
and by pure strength of his
uncompromising beliefs
he thought he had progress defeated,
even before the battle cry of rational thought
could be once again heard across the waves of history –
waves that would inexorably collide with the shores of our moment.

Jenny Campbell

Terror Australis

I

The Southern Land – where snow but rarely falls –
In Yuletide brings the threat of searing fire;
Where sun and heat with sweat and dust conspire –
No holly and no ivy deck the halls.
The ground is shrouded here with naught but dust
And – scorched beneath the sun's incessant glare –
The sheep that dully raise their heads and stare
May die of thirst; the barbed-wire fences rust.

The celebration of the birth of Christ
Is shadowed here by legends dark and old;
The nights can be both comforting and cold
The days string out like rope, knotted and spliced.
It is an alien land, where Christmas cheer
Gives way to trepidation and to fear.

II

A land of painted cabalistic signs
That lead us into pitiless vast space,
Where near and far and dark and light change place,
While jagged serpents dance along our spines.
Ghosts dwell here of an unrelenting kind –
Survivors of the famine and the flood,
Which rob them of their last remains of food –
Thrice-vicious ghosts that prey upon the mind.

A land whose secrets yield and break apart
To only those who live and die alone
(Perhaps condemned by pointing of the bone)
And see the truth at last in its dead heart.
Horrors half-glimpsed through waves of scorching light
Give way to freezing, arid, taunting night.

III

A Christmas here is not a northern Yule –
Hot foetid winds defeat the gasping breath;
The arid sands give warning of stark death;
The ocean's roar portends a fate most cruel.
Did Lovecraft dream, in 'The Shadow Out of Time'
A tenth of all the burning, torpid fear –
The horrors that inimical lie here
In wait for dwellers in this alien clime?

Antipodean nightmares strange and bleak
Fill dreamers' minds with eerie visions dire,
That fill their souls with recondite desire
And draw them on to leer and shout and shriek.
Oppressed and tortured, baneful and malign,
With their grim fate Australians must entwine.

Leigh Blackmore

A Deathless Love

Were you the beast
red ochres dripping from your maw
as I conjured you to graze closer closer
fusing your shaggy horned head over my frail body
beast and hunter   hunter beast?
Was it my spirit or yours
that crumbled in the heat   exhausted   spent
succumbing to a union so intense?

Was I the priestess   you the priest
dragging a traveller's wearied feet across desert sands
to that place where rivers meet under date palms
stripped naked   fevered cold   we could barely show restraint?
Was it my spirit or yours
that knelt and kissed the serpent's languid head
and vowed we would not part again?

Was I the magus   you the whore
that shared the cup of absinthe   lip to lip
invoking ecstasy to breathe a demons breath
waking blind and shaken and estranged?
How did we part that day
to lose our way through London's cobbled streets
and never meet again?

Was I the witch   you the urban mage
crossing paths in corridors   in bookstores or cafés
wondering where we'd met or what was that scent
of blood, of desert palms, of night's indulgence?

Is it my spirit or yours that stills
long enough to breathe in present and past lives
and recognise the light of recognition in each others eyes?

Margaret Curtis

Dumpling

Friendship, when lack of communication,
Becomes a dumpling in boiling soup,
Too hot to get close,
Too round to go straight,
Too short to last long,
Too much wrapped up to read the mind,
Too steamy to understand,
Too messed up to clarify,
Too fragile to keep intact.

The dumpling of friendship, when broken,
Is sometimes as sweet as a lover's kitchen,
Sometimes as sour as an embarrassed heart,
Other times as distant as strangers are.

Oh, dumpling of friendship,
Please stay where you are,
While you are still fresh and alive,
Give us pleasure, give us life!

Cherie

A Tamil Mother's Laugh!

It's not a skeleton on stilts!
The stride of a scrawny woman
Anguish engraved on her face
Urgency gives gait purpose
Swiftly, she reaches Chemmani
A cemetery filled with 'mass graves'
Her son rests here with other 'terrorists'
Euphemism for 'Tamils' in Sri Lanka
She laughed!

An arch at a distance
A raven offers a harsh cry
A sentry post; hidden by sandbags
She turns and briskly walks
Direction different though path the same
Again ancient temple in her sight
Head failed to tilt, sign of disrespect!
Here once she prayed; made offerings
Not now!
She laughed!

She knew soldiers kidnapped her son
Tortured, killed and dumped at Chemmani
A pantheon of deities remains listless
Like the vicious state
A dereliction of duty!
She laughed!

Bhagavadas Sriskanthadas

Letter from Oz

his blue/white aerogramme arrived
tattered and soggy from the rain
the local postman curious of its origins
as he delivered my mail, the dogs barking
he hurried away on his bicycle muttering in Bahasa
as I opened the mail hurriedly a photograph of my future husband
falls out of the envelope with a clipping of the ad
from our local paper *The New Straits Times* wanted penfriend
for young-at-heart widower, 'mutual love, companionship
happy-go-lucky, tall, suntanned, debonair Aussie'
a naïve young Asian woman who just wanted a better life
in the 'Lucky Country'
a year later her dreams and aspirations shattered
a nightmare journey of child custody, homeless, depression
ugly divorce – later emerging
like a phoenix from the ashes
freedom to be 'ME'

Dona Samson Zappone

Marriage

'Detective Darwin,' his wife would muse
as he sloshed in heavy-headed, mind-leaded from his room
'have you any extraordinary news, any vexing but enchanting clues
for me? A new barnacle perhaps, a perplexing addition
to your family tree we marine-wives at tea
teasingly call your Monster & Co? Though we don't mind
the slime of innuendo, or the wild surmising
when you & your heretical friends
(although I do like the chutney that Mr Hooker sends)
preach undersea reproduction
the stalks & sacks & budding of creatures;
we do not mind Mr *Arthrobalanus*, your devious little barnacle,
nor the fact that you seem to be
increasingly cirripede-like (I have noticed your whiskers
waving at me), or even that you light your room
with luminous zoophytes at night
but I have been bothered by these strange constant leaks
of saltwater under doors
& do not speak of hermaphrodites
& doubles penes &c &c over the soup please,
at the very least when the children are present.'

'Don't be cross at me dear wife & cousin Em, life is a contest
of forces, a Hegelian joust. Let the strongest forces
by their strength survive, & the weakest forms, well you see…
& you, my sweet, are the perfect example
of the emergence of beauty
(though not order) from the struggle to be.

But I know you will wish me & my barnacles *al Diabolo*
when you hear of the half-inch female species, Mrs Ibla,
I found today, whose body, like a jacket, has two pockets
each manned by a tiny husband, & would you believe
what I do, that 'embedded in the flesh of their wives
they pass their whole lives…as testis, mere bags of spermatozoa
& can never move again?' But I shan't say
a word more about it, will upset you, except that I sense
my truth is a virtue & these minute males are truly
wonderful. Evidence that my species theory
(like confessing a murder I know) is *gospel*.

'It takes no quick work to know
that the wonder & riddle is one such as she,'
Emma said, '(the stronger sex indeed!)
who will put up with two useless, purple, sack-like chaps
affixed to her skirts & her bed for eternity without rest?
Asexual sprouting, or whatnot, no matter,
this cannot make for feminine happiness
with or without Heaven
but only proves as *gospel* what I, Emma,
dutiful and true, already knew:
that man & wife being constantly together for life
should have its limits.
Don't try to unseat me with your lance, dear Charley,
I have already budded seven for you.'

Emily Ballou

Small Beginnings

It was the hardest thing I did in my life
cracked my heart in two you said
leave four small children at the gate
turn and step into the old black Ford.

I can travel with you now
I sit beside the brown suitcase in the back seat
torrents of tears flowing, your gaunt face promising
one day you will return to us.

Two years of our lives you lost
an iron will steered you back
complete with an ocean of love
that kissed the shores of all our lives for all our days.

Soon I will be twice the age you were when you departed.
Now I am the tallest of them all
then the smallest
and part of me stands
still at the gate
one hand inside my trousers pocket
the other in a brother's hand
the old black Ford splutters into life
moves through the avenue of beech trees
disappears behind the high hedge
falls over the edge of the earth.

Maurice Whelan

Greenwich Village (1980)

I saw the light appear
he took off his shirt
he looked through the window
as if to say, 'Hello,
I see you are home.'
Flirtations across the street.
Maybe, I'll stand at the window
for a while, have a beer or two,
and watch your loneliness
each night.
You look fine from afar.
I cannot see your tears.

Barvara Hush

Pointy Toes

Pointy toes
Pointing up
White billowing skirts
A tease, a flirt
Ripples, frills below
White satin sheen
Criss-cross seams
Dance your toes upon the sky
Look up high
Spread your skirts out wide
The orchestra inside
Makes music
You want to dance and glide

WHAT is it?
THE Sydney OPERA HOUSE

Carol Nelson

2010

With our twentieth birthday on the horizon we opened this season with Sheryl Persson's *Scarcely Random* poetry title from Ginninderra Press. In her interview, Sheryl also talked about her non-fiction works (one of them dealt with contagious diseases), her work with Diverse group of poets (addressing paintings and other art works with poems and so on) and the painting vs poetry dynamic generally. She was also applying to become Auburn's first Poet Laureate (and succeeded!).

Tatiana Bonch was on hand to talk about the Antipodes Russian Festival where Auburn Poets and Writers Group and numerous others would perform on a webinar cross to Moscow – and get to see Muscovite poets *in situ* in return.

During the supper break, coincidentally or otherwise, many people seemed to be comparing their stories about journeys to far-flung places. This was led by Dianne (a long-time regular of LP) and her recent visit to Russia and Central Asia.

The smaller group in the sitting room after supper looked at Words Walking in Wilderness: poets as explorers (and frequently ne'er do wells!) rather than makers as the ancient Greeks had defined wordsmiths. This convenor had just come back from an emblematic seven-day trek in south-west Tasmania – completing a circuit to remote Lost World Plateau started ten years previously. I read 'Lineage', the only poem I penned en route.

A young lady recently back from working and travelling overseas came in just to case the joint. Her name was Rima and she was soon to join Auburn Poets and Writers in performance. The Gig Guide at the start of the show announced a new venue, a Mexican café in Enmore which Running Order (Danny, Bill and Maureen from Live Poets) would later perform at; Mario Cabrera was the poetry MC.

The Russians came in force in March to hear Tatiana Bonch read her work and contemporary Russian writers in translation. She also provided a quirky account in the pre-performance interview of how she happens upon her material.

It was heartening to see the likes of the indefatigable Nora Krouk attend Don Bank again after so many years. This evening had started with the accomplished poet and teacher of writing, Mark Tredinnick, generous in his insights in interview before giving a very strong reading. Apart from the birthday party, this was the largest audience at Live Poets over the year. Peter Wagner led off with a poem from Les Murray's new book *Taller When Prone*.

April was our twentieth birthday, celebrated with balloons and memory boards of photos and memorabilia from past Live Poets gatherings. There was also a rousing performance by folk/blues duo Buck and Deanne, previewing their new album.

A massive open section – roughly in chronological order of people reading at Live Poets over twenty years – followed, spliced with episodes in 'the history of' and such topics as 'What is a Live Poet?', memorable guest spots, comic and poignant moments, the weirdest presentations – and when does a poetry venue become a little more than that?

The sitting room was so full with people sitting on the floor that several others had to crane their necks from the back door or the kitchen – or listen hard over a drink in the courtyard. North Sydney Leisure director Martin Ellis passed someone his camera so they could get a shot of the goings-on for the council newsletter.

Buck and Deanne's slot ended with them sharing the stage with Frank Ebzury, chorusing on 'Little Black Bed Bug', about an unfortunate night Frank, as a travelling salesman, spent in a motel in Bredbo, Snowy Mountains.

In the courtyard then there was a literary quiz – questions pulled from the riddle barrel, with winners invited to karaoke. The After Party was captured by Bill Tibben and his roving cinema verité camera – the entire evening on film would be edited for general video release on the occasion of our twenty-first birthday in April 2011.

There were inevitably quieter times in May, with Jess Cook providing one of her character inhabitations before our eyes. We really didn't know what would come next. She also gave an impressive interview about the performance principle and the work of Token Imagination (a cooperative company of which she is a principal) in bringing poetry to wider, nay weirder, audiences. There was one occasion, for instance, when its performers invaded the city centre in a sort of word storm, wearing costumes emblazoned with various bizarre words.

After supper, Fadeel Kayat stood by to bring us pictures from the UN project to return the Marsh Arabs – Fadeel's tribe and family – to the land Saddam Hussein uprooted them from in the 1990s. This story deserves a much wider audience and Fadeel's simple, powerful poems should be put between covers as soon as possible.

Phyliss Perlstone, originally from the USA, was our guest in June. It's not easy to describe the form or effect of Phyliss's poetry, a series of rhythmic phrases – 'abstract paintings of words' an onlooker described it as this night – which is apposite, as Phyliss is also a visual artist. Hers is a rare talent that amuses as it instructs.

After supper we looked at song lyrics as poetry with Lee Cass providing first-hand experience of that concept/conundrum. Examples from the pop/rock world surveyed included the work of the Beatles, Lou Reed, Don Mclean, Simon and Garfunkel and David Bowie – the gamut of applications including 'I am the Walrus', 'The Bewlay Brothers', 'Kids', 'Poem on the Underground Wall' and the riotous 'On the Amazon'.

July was billed as a Winter Words Festival with an expanded program. First up, the inimitable and syntax-savvy poet and teacher Les Wicks, who made several cogent observations in his short interview and gave us poetry in 3D – principally from his *Ambrosiacs* and *Stories From the Feet* books that leave grit under the fingernails.

There was a look at literature in the erstwhile current edition of the Sydney art Biennale and our two guests from Melbourne – the Road Trip poets (but not in frill-necked shirts 'like the troubadours of old' as the local paper wagged), Steve Smart, whom many consider the best performance poet in Australia, and the irascible, pith-helmeted Randall Stephens, fresh from African conquests! (No, wait – cancel that! Steve Smart had written Randall's bio too!)

This night also saw the inaugural Monologue Challenge, where contestants pulled the speech of a major play – from ancient Greek tragedy to Shakespeare to Arthur Miller and Samuel Beckett – out of a hat and had to instantly make that role a part of them! The brave contestants were Jane Reynolds, Peter Wagner, David Falcon and Bob Howe, while Bill Tibben ceded his participation to Randall Stephens, who assumed the role of a motivating drunk at a famous Greek soldier's funeral, urging on his mates around the wineskin, and took it home as his new overcoat.

August saw a revisit to the 2003 Live Poets' Press production of *Open Boat – Barbed Wire Sky*, with a newly arranged program of twelve poems taking us from nightmarish journeys by mountain and sea to incarceration in the dubious paradise of a cage in the Australian outback. This convenor opened this section with a new poem, 'Double Shore', and the poems which followed were 'Journey' (from Assad Cina), 'Light Continent' (Maureen Ten), 'Crochet at the Bus Stop' (Penelope Grace), 'Second Language' (Lesley Fowler), 'Razor Wire' (Jenni Nixon), 'Government is Unmoved' (Terril George), 'What Rhymes with Injustice?' (Les Wicks), 'Apathy' (John Weerden),' Just Visiting' (Jacqueline Buswell), 'From a Villawood Detainee' (Mohsen Soltanyzand) and 'Unequal Distribution' (Caroline Lowry).

There was a special reading by Nashaa (a member of Auburn Poets and Writers). Nashaa is a veteran of the refugee process who survived Baxter to gain her citizenship and later argue against the government's refugee policy in the streets of Auburn in the SWF production *Colours in Waiting*.

It was the first visit to Don Bank of George Clarke, later to become an inspiring regular. This convenor closed the night with Craig Powell's 'Poem as a Place' from *Open Boat*, which touched on the concerns of identity and place particularly for indigenous Australians.

Proceeds from the sales of *Open Boat* are directed to the House of Welcome (HOW), Carramar. Its director Cyril O'Connor was on hand to tell us about the facility's critical assistance to asylum-seekers in times of need in a new country. The $200 dollars collected this night took the total *Open Boat* has raised to $8,200. Cyril later printed 'Double Shore' on the first page of the next HOW newsletter.

After supper, Running Order – the performance poetry trio of Maureen Ten, Bill Tibben and Danny Gardner – did thirty minutes of poets reading separately, poets reading together and reflecting on common themes.

September saw poet, novelist, former art critic and book reviewer, and convenor of Sappho Bookshop Readings, Roberta Lowing, reading from her book *Ruin*. This was based on four voices from the Iraq war. Roberta proved her authenticity by portraying an American GI's view of his chosen function overseas with Iraqi native Nashaa, in a headscarf, eyeballing her utterances from the front row.

The second half of the night – to honour the UN Year of Diversity – featured Oral Poetry from the First Peoples: poems from a tradition not written down originally but sung around the communal fire in ceremonies, and so on. People in the audience nominated which of the world's peoples they wished to represent in a process Roberta described as organic and unique among poetry venues of her experience. She joined in with her reading of a speech of a Somali praise singer, 'The Limits of Submission'.

This convenor read a translated Mongol poem (about excessive drinking!); Nur Alam read a poem from the Malay, 'Oh that My love were in My Arms'; Danny read 'Be not Proud of your Sweet Body' from the Gondi; Bob Howe read 'Eshu – the God of Fish', translated from the Yoruba; Danny did the 'Song of the Caribou' from the Inuit, Eskimo; Frank Ebzury's partner read 'Yellow Bus Stop' from Brazil and 'Sunrise Dance' from the American Indian; 'The Famine Song' from the old Irish was read by Bill Tibben. There was an old creation chant in Maori and Ann Jarjoura read an Australian Aboriginal song cycle. Danny read 'Down in the Valley' as the English contribution.

In the open section, Frank Ebzury read three poems from Aboriginal activists of their time – Jack Davis, Kevin Gilbert and Colin Johnston – while Bill Tibben reflected on 'The Smell of Humans'.

October offered another contrast in styles with Pakistani-born poet Nur Alam, a former customer services director of Westpac and instrumental in the formation of Auburn Poets and Writers Group (five years young in September), reading her moving, often quirky investigations into human habits and social nature. She had a book in preparation for publication – the striking cover design by her son adorned the LP PR leaflet for October.

The already small crowd had shrunk somewhat to hear the presentation of Spanish classical guitar and bass in the hands of Bolivian Gilmar Munoz and Juan Medellin born in Brazil. This eclectic, often playful, interaction of darkly accented picking took us away to other worlds.

In the open, George Clarke read a piece called 'Over the Divide', which resonated, while Ava Banerjee's 'Education' was influenced by William Blake motifs.

We reverted to a home grown theme in November with a night called The Country Comes to the City. Jim Low was down from the mountains to launch his new CD, *Above the Creek Bed*, while Brian Bell from out west brought yarns and insight to the table; a good spin somewhere between homily and social satire. Jim's music was on the airwaves as people came in. The structures are endearing and the melodies stick in the mind. Jim interspersed his music with reflections on his past working life in North Sydney. Brian asked us to listen closely to his more serious side but he continually distracted with his facility for corny throwaways.

For locals there was the added bonus of us tracing facets of Henry Lawson's time in the area via the Walk and Talk notes from the North Sydney Heritage Centre's History Week event. Lawson poems touched on here included 'The Old Horse Ferry', 'The Pub that Lost its License', 'The Pride of the Flu' and 'Above Lavender Bay'. The tour notes included anecdotal accounts of 'Lawson lurching about the street' (from Jean Blundell's memoirs of 'that man going to and from the shambles').

Thanks were due to North Sydney historian Ian Hoskins. It was while he and I were discussing an S.T. Gill painting – that

I believe must have been worked up from the spot Don Bank looked out on and down to the harbour in 1861 – that gave me the idea of including Lawson's North Shore to further our theme this night.

The open section – under the loose title of Poems from our Blood's Country (to evoke dear Judith Wright) – saw Janet Reynolds read 'Andy's Gone with Cattle'.

After supper, I read two letters from the State Library of NSW archives written by Lawson. One asking for money from friends in Brisbane, and this to his 'employer' (publisher): 'Dear Mr Robertson. Please lend me a shilling to get home with. Yours ever, Henry Lawson.' One more poem from Lawson from 1917 closed the evening. This one was written in another bout of reactionary behaviour – attacking the proposed coal loader facility in 'The Sacrifice of Ball's Head'. It was a brisk morning's walk from where Lawson then lived. Today, the coal loader is being developed into a centre for sustainability.

Transported

after the painting *Circular Quay*, 2009, by Kevin Connor

From the dark the ghost ships still sail to the quay
convicts in their barrel bellies.
Beneath the well-scrubbed boards
it is endless night. Tar oozes
from the ship's seams and the sea weeps salt tears.
No pleasure craft these, despite their names
>> *The Friendship*
>> *The Golden Grove*
>> HMS *Supply*

And the lost souls who went into the sea
whether at five bells or eight
in the silent deep they drift like swaying kelp
their sail-shrouds floating loose about them
no eyes to pierce the prism that distorts
the solid spheres of one man's dream – above.

As oily opal water ripples at the stone steps
sighing, sighing her name, Elizabeth
the spirit of her brittle-boned body slips past.
I hear the rustle of fine fabric
imagine her black hell and seven years
for a petticoat of silk.

But long after the floggings and the hunger
a legacy of flotillas, soaring sails, horizons and endless light.

Sheryl Persson

My Darling, It's Late

My darling, it's late, it's almost one. Light
rain like flywire keeps the summer night hanging,
and the humid early hour's an unwelcome suitor
at my door. My lonely Corona's drunk now
and my head's been sipping gin; my legs are lead
from leading me astray. Bed would be a quest
I'd leave on any minute were you in it,
but you're not; nor is your phone, it seems, in voice
or close at hand. No matter: let me fling a million kisses
at the five wide-open windows of your soul; then let me
find a book of hours and let me sit and slowly
turn its pages into gecko song until my melancholy suitor
slips away. For it's late, my love, and almost one,
and this is how I miss you, till I'm almost done.

Mark Tredinnick

In the time of war

when we will never meet again
and will not fall in love
I see now how you see it
this bald man his cheeks dozing hugging an orange backpack
this old man with protruding lip reading a Moscow newspaper
    Civil War begun in Ukraine
slowly he turns pages back and forth without stopping for one
this girl bearishly cross-legged jeans jacket and maroon nail polish
a man in black baggy coat his narrow mouth
this woman with a brooch the low-cut neckline and boots
fashionable sleeveless fur coat

each of us
asleep and in a hurry
cowardly
envious
evil
but you do know
we are
in fact
still
alive

                                                   Tatiana Bonch-Osmolovskaya

Call Waiting

I tried to call but you were out.
I tried again, I tried throughout
the dreary hours
six, seven, eight
while time drags on, and time grows late.
I wait and hope and wait and then
I call again and yet your phone
is cruel still,
confounds my will,
in silence till,
a wordless signal's sent
I see that love for you has captured me.
The two of us, the you and I
so long awaited, long frustrated,
clearly fated to be mated.
Yet still apart, still separate
you have my heart.
But you are
late.

So what of me?
I want you so, I want you so,
to talk, to hold, to kiss, to know.
But you're not home to get that phone
and I'm alone and lonely too
and thinking 'where oh where are you?'
So hurry back and have your shower
eat your food within the hour.
For when I call my love
(that's you)
the day is not quite hued in blue.

But rainbow – toned and sunny-bright
luminous – the not of night.
The disembodied voice I hear
is still your soul, my dear, my dear.
So don't be late.
Don't make me wait.
Unlatch the gate that makes me pay
with anxious sighs, impatient thoughts
uneasy feelings, restless dealings
edgy visions, troubled foresight
and the other familiar fears of lovers on their own.
Just please be there.
Pick up your phone.

Ava Banerjee

Mothers

for my mother

Another mother smiled at me today
As we passed in the street. A quiet smile
Though total strangers, she had seen the glow
Of gentle recognition as my eyes embraced
Her tiny babe, safe-tied with love against her breast.
Her 'now' my 'yesterday'.

Carolyn Lowry

Their eyes disturb us

The old moon has quartered itself. Its cratered eye plays on our minds to think of an ancient sameness. I am in dismay at being dependent on things always as they are. The gaze of someone who will not swerve, even to answer why, gives us the pang of what is not possible now. We are in the grip of something. What does this mean? We are held by a power, held by people we do not trust. Their eyes disturb us. They are murderous. What does that mean? It is hard to describe. It is in their purpose. And they are a collective. Yet these eyes have different faces. They belong to separate people. Sometimes they are steady like everlasting things or squinting in an obedience of the moment. Or they are beseeching, waving their ideas in our faces. Putting forward their worst intentions. As if we'll be dazzled by their candour.

Phyllis Perlstone

Hindered by the Hearth

Leave our doors
step
with weight
stop on a tickle
check the mailbox (you do know
it's the middle of a long weekend?) back upstairs
to verify the heater is cold have you
got your wallet this
leaving will take a while,
maybe have a cup of coffee?
We work hard to fill the question.

Jowled sky
about the courtesies of coal
you say the day is *leaden*
leading nowhere
the whimlost winter,
this breeder of night,
is subtle. I will convince myself.
Our tracksuits are smeared with belief.

Les Wicks

NYC – poetry bars

No really it's a poetry bar
Monday to Sunday – poetry
sometimes bands or plays
get to play second fiddle
poetry is always the headline act

NYC – closing times
There are no laws in New York City
that say bars must ever close

The trains run all night
you will never have to wait
for a cab on a city street

Avoid the fortune teller on East 3rd St
the only fortune she's interested in
is her own, she's a thief and a liar

NYC Times Square
A Times Square hotdog
does not a meal make

in crowded neon
this is not my New York
still I'm glad that I went
and saw for myself

Steve Smart

sorry

…I'm really sorry

it's time
for me to be more
than just the words I use

for me to make the effort
to meet you
no more halfways

I've dropped my terms
no longer looking
waiting asking hoping
for a fix
just a mark to get past this

our journey ends here
not in Paris
not in Melbourne
the only place you need to get to
is forgiveness

…I will go the rest of the way

Randall Stephens

The Donation

I stare at ten red fingernails spread on arm boards
fine blonde hair too real for the pillow
eyes roam monitors, oxygen level,
heartbeat pulse, return to red, back to clock,
move behind the unwind of minutes.

She's 16, fell from her horse
will never know the wind again,
draped in sterile sheets
arms are free strapped in a 'v'
little red arrows pointing.

Hung in this strung space
each second cuts silence.

Time is patient, but, nevertheless.
How long will it take
too long, for thoughts to haunt ideas,
the inevitable has already been crossed
if the earth spun any faster
it could not change this outcome.

I'm gloved, untouchable,
even my breath is masked
had I held one manicured hand,
would it have mattered?

At last, the needles are dropping
I pick up the scalpel. She's run out of everything
this girl has already left. Vital signs are not her own
machines waiting for switches to be thrown.

Her falter took fifty minutes. Now is the speed.
We swoop. Taloned crows on offal. Place organs into ice,
surrendered for survival of strangers.

The family have lost a child,
ours is a task more brutal than grief.
There is no debriefing.
What I take home, follows.

Susan Adams

Seeds of Change

'All things hang like a drop of dew…' – W.B. Yeats

The perfume of the sweetest fruit
        contains the scent of decay,
fullness of ambition, abandoning youth
        forever left on the far shore.

A giant flamboyant poppy
        paper petals and black heart,
full and giving, orange flamenco skirts
        soon to drift and fall.

Vines, orange yellow after yielding
        nature's sweet sun scented gift,
nurtured for man's sustenance and song
        during frost brittle winter.

The valley a story of summer
        held in the palm of time's hand,
and geology will slowly metamorphose
        this gift wrapped world

into something not so familiar.

George Clark

By Ourselves, Nothing?

I search my files
the future map
there are no answers

Maybe
we can advance as far west as we want
but the faces never change
the creased hands raised
against the sun and our unwinking eye
> *come with us we say*
> *we will honour your secrets*

but they edge away
to their land of hard rocks
and scorpions which display devils' tails
in the corner of the goat's dry eye

they see the shadows flaring into parachutes
pitch forks into guns
villages enclosed by honeycombed walls of skulls
the knowledge of everything
one man will do to another
> *come with us*
> *we need to see your inner rooms*

but he grips the wooden fence
and puts up his hand
to block out
the rock-falls of sun
and the metallic gaze that will disappear him
      (he knows this from a millennia of discussions
in mule-breath dawns
just as he knows to back away

from white paper and red wax seals)
>*come with us*
>*we must dissect the chambers of your heart*

and he did
that other man
sun-creased and wide-eyed

and when he couldn't raise his punctured hands
we said
come with us
into our dark caverns
come be imprinted
with the black and white collapse of our lives.

Roberta Lowing

Dis Place

Dis place or that place, it is all the same,
We're under God's sky, it's his you exclaim!
No longer in one place but home is another,
Dis place or that place, were you my brother?
We roam hungry and desperate, far and wide,
Hounded from our homes, are you on my side?
Those children left to fend all on their own,
No mother, lost father, only pictures are shown.
Dis place or that, it is all the same
I remain, worse than animal, I am shamed.
Displaced in that where I have no claim or success,
Rights of generations wiped out, no rights of egress.
Dis placed into that where they say I am to blame,
Human I am, will be and wish to remain.
Please help me for my family I deeply implore,
Don't send me away or show me the door.
Dis place or that, it is all the same,
WE are all God's children destined for the flame.

Nur J Alam

In Between Fairytales

There's no burst of energy lighting my smile,
no push to achieve, and no bubble of joy.
My colourful glow has been gone for a while.
The tiniest trickle can really annoy.
Though evenings are long, I will make it somehow.
I'm in between fairy tales, just for now.

I'm not going out to the Saturday dance,
no bowling or movies, just work through the night.
My mind is repeating each grim circumstance,
those desperate dramas in stark black and white.
It ended when love took its very last bow.
I'm in between fairy tales, just for now.

Returning once more to the depth of my pain,
with negative thoughts taking hold of my mind,
the phrases repeat till they drive me insane –
I search for a method to leave it behind.
The whole thing began with the tiniest row
and I'm in between fairy tales, just for now.

Asking my heart why it all had to be –
most people seem happy meandering by.
Illusory thoughts that it's probably me
bring thunderous clouds to a luminous sky.
So why can't I see through the shallowest vow?
I'm in between fairy tales, just for now.

Perhaps in the finish my world will be fine,
with love shining out from that cavernous pit.
Once I discover the love that is mine,
with nobody sharing the tiniest bit.
I look forward to joys that a life can endow,
but I'm in between fairy tales, just for now.

Brian Bell

Poetry and Presenting it in Public
Part Three

Is it good/natural to be nervous when you are reading/performing poetry?

Benito di Fonzo: Yes. Everybody gets stage fright. John Lennon used to vomit out of nervousness before he went on stage. Shirley Bassey needs a double cognac before she can even consider it. Actors have all sorts of things they do, from yoga to cocaine, to get themselves on stage. I remember an English performance poet once telling me that after his one-thousandth performance he stopped getting stage fright, but I didn't believe him. Of course you can numb yourself with beta blockers but, having tried that, I find it just kills the entire energy of the performance. And you lose the post-stage high afterwards. The pre-stage fear and the post-stage high are in direct proportion to one another, so dig the fear and use its energy – it's the fermentation process.

Candy Royalle: Absolutely. Well-managed nerves are nothing more than adrenalin. Adrenalin makes you sharp. Harness it.

Richard James Allen: A bit of nervousness keeps you sharp.

Scott Sandwich: Damn right. Enjoy your nervousness. It's such a specific feeling, you have to learn to love and embrace nerves! Having said that, once you make nerves a part of your performance, you stop calling them 'nerves' and it just becomes energy. Use it, because if you don't have enough energy for one poem, then you should be performing something else. I'm such an idealist like that; if you're not having fun, then the audience won't be having any, either, and then no one wants to be there.

David Falcon: I don't think it is bad to be nervous. The best thing to do is to share it with the audience. They want you to succeed and letting them know this little bit about yourself helps to soothe the nerves and get the audience even more on side.

Philip Radmall: As long as you use it positively and channel your nerves into concentration.

Susan Adams: It's natural but not necessarily good – although some respond better when under stress.

Erwin Zehentner: There are ways of combating them. My favourite method before a race was to shut my eyes and think of nothing. People were walking past saying, 'Look at this guy, he's fast asleep!' Not quite. Get your plan for your reading into your head and concentrate on that. Getting nervous increases your adrenalin level. A horse for instance pumps two hundred litres of blood per minute at full speed and produces more adrenalin than it can use up.

Martin Langford: Most Australian performances are too low-key to elicit much nervousness.

Paul Buckberry: Nerves are over-rated. All nerves can be traced to insecurities, lack of confidence, even an over-important need to please, of wanting to be good and thereby accepted. Expectations can be dangerous, allowing the mind to wander towards the periphery of 'what if…' Preconceived ideas or notions of a particular end result. All these things and more can be traced back to pre-show jitters.

Willem Tibben: Good/natural yes…but not past a certain point. Loss of control or being nervous enough to be distracted by one's own reading – as one is reading.

Les Wicks: It's certainly common.

Cathy Bray: I have been doing Sydney Fringe festivals of my preambles and poems since 2010. I was mystified and relieved to find at my first show, I didn't have a nervous bone in my body. I put this down to the freedom of being in a Fringe festival, the confidence I had that I was reading and writing truthfully and the fact that I had the full script and poems in my hands – which avoided the stress of possibly forgetting lines.

Edwin Wilson: I still have strong memories of what would have been my third professional gig, the first time I ever read at Live Poets in 1990 – after the publication of *Songs of the Forest* (Hale and Iremonger), in a restaurant in Neutral Bay. My wife had come along for a 'free' meal with me prior to my having to 'sing for my supper'. I had been suffering from a degree of performance anxiety. Then when I was being introduced I was very thrown by a young man in the audience who was glaring at me with unconcealed malice, whose body language implied he was thinking why was it me up there at the podium with a book of poems from a 'real' publisher and not him? Believe me, it had been one hell of a haul to get that book published! The light was shining in my eyes as well and I could hardly see the writing on the page! Luckily, I'd had experience of talking to groups and I cracked a lame joke about live poets being better than the alternative. I fell back into a kind of default automatic mode – and did not completely disgrace myself!

Are there any things too naked to bring to the table when you perform/read?

Candy Royalle: Absolutely not.

Susan Adams: No, only poor poems expressing emotion badly.

Cathy Bray: Of course – anything that injures yourself and others by its reading is 'too naked'. The former is self-harming or masochistic and the latter may be cruel or embarrassing.

Les Wicks: Yes. Both from the perspective of leaving the poet too vulnerable/injured and knowing that a degree of nuance is lost when a poem is read some pieces may be read entirely out of context by the audience. But I don't believe the reader should shy away from 'hard' subjects.

Martin Langford: The nakedness of one's desire to be approved for one's poetry should definitely not be brought to the reading. For the rest, there are no subjects inherently impossible, but it can be extremely difficult to find the right way to bring some things to the table.

Kate Lilley: There could be – it's personal.

Erwin Zehentner: Some aspects of relationships, sexuality or politics should remain under the table unless the reading is specific to the topic in question.

Willem Tibben: Too naked? Absolutely. But this varies from poet to poet and from audience to audience – there are things I would read in some places but not others. For example, 'The Smell of Cows' Number Two'. To get it into an anthology I agreed to an edit – a movement of one line from one place in the poem to another – from someone other than the editor. Then at the launch I was asked to not read 'that one'. Clearly it had the capacity to offend some or at least make them uncomfortable – and it wasn't worth the hassle to resist or to defy. Okay, so I am a poetwhore!

David Falcon: I am not so uninhibited as to be prepared to bare all for my art. So yes, there are definitely things that I would not put into my poetry. They are likely to cause embarrassment to people who love me.

Paul Buckberry: This is a question of time and place and mood. Some poems will inevitably embarrass some listeners. Audiences should be prepared for that, not the other way around.

Richard James Allen: It's a personal choice.

Edwin Wilson: Poetic bitching is a form of self ranking on the greasy pole of Literature. As a general rule of thumb, it should be off-limits to say nasty things in verse about other poets – or one's spouse. And because of my generation – born 1942 – I tend to feel slightly embarrassed for the spouses of female poets exploring their sexuality.

Scott Sandwich: It's up to you what you present to an audience. You just have to decide what you want them to experience. If you want them to feel uncomfortable, do it. I personally treat my audiences like people – people I'm actually meeting and engaging in conversation. I don't say things that I wouldn't say if I met them in an elevator. This doesn't mean I can't challenge them, or confront them, because if I want to, I can. There are plenty of artists – great artists, mind you – who don't want to invite their audiences in. But me? I'm on that stage making friends, earning trust. I'm not manipulating anyone, I'm just showing people who I am, telling stories, spreading joy, expressing anger, arguing a point, or sharing sadness.

Can reading poetry to an audience be taught?

Cathy Bray: You can't fake sincerity but, just as acting can be taught, there are certain basic skills which can be taught to make the reading of poetry out loud to an audience more enjoyable.

Paul Buckberry: Probably. It helps to have a touch of the thespian about you, a desire in the first place to perform. Teaching a performer to have fun is a whole other issue. Personally, if it isn't fun for the performer, it will be a struggle to teach them to read poetry aloud.

Candy Royalle: Yes. I do so in my own workshops. Mostly people need help with confidence and some basic skills to ensure that they are doing their work justice.

Les Wicks: There certainly are a few pointers, common mistakes a new reader makes.

Kate Lilley: Yes – up to a point.

Erwin Zehentner: If you go to readings, you should, given we all have a level of intelligence, pick up on something, and become reasonably proficient.

Benito di Fonzo: To a degree – if not as a degree. You can teach stage skills, public reading skills, voice projection, timing. But it seems to come naturally to the best of them.

Martin Langford: It can be taught up to the point where the reader's understanding of the poem starts to falter. All the rules of entertainment apply across all art forms – including poetry.

Susan Adams: There are aspects of it that can be taught.

Edwin Wilson: Poets are both born and made. There are technical aspects that can be taught to assist with reading poetry to an audience but the poetic spirit is essentially innate and probably can't be taught.

Richard James Allen: How to warm up your voice, how to stand, how to speak, how to project, how to use a mike, how to include the audience in your gaze and gesture, how to order your reading, how to listen to the audience's responses to vary what you have planned if necessary – they can all be taught. Can true talent be taught? Probably not. But talent requires knowledge and technique and feedback and practice and skill and patience and encouragement and resilience to flourish.

David Falcon: Like any activity, technique in reading poetry is something that can be learned and improved upon.

Phil Radmall: The actual specific voice of the poet can never be taught.

Scott Sandwich: Can it be taught? Definitely – though you can teach yourself. Just do it more.

Willem Tibben: But some people have more natural ability.

2011

February started the ball rolling with the return of a favourite – Tug Dumbly, longtime master of Australian spoken word, who delighted with his moods, from classics like 'Road Kill' to 'My Ordinary Australians' (thank you, Kevin!). From the childish misunderstood ingenue to the belligerent monster rampant in 'I Like it Strong!' His interview took us through his performance history and even helped us unravel the mystery of his name.

Ray and Eva turned up – last seen at TAP Gallery, the place where Tug got his start. We had so many people booking tickets for this one. No one left early and open section readers were few.

March saw something very special – a celebration of Mary Tang's work culminating in her migrant stories' project with William Yang that had recently galvanised the Chinese New Year Festival and Parramatta's Riverside Theatre. Mary's many supporters meant another sell-out crowd. A person came to film Mary's interview and reading – her spotlights would have fried the front row of the crowd and I persuaded her they weren't necessary!

Our other guest – rapper and winner of the 2008 Australian Poetry Slam, Omar Musa – arrived fresh off a bus from Canberra (he had asked me to forward him the fare in advance) and in the first half was plainly out of his comfort zone looking around as though it was a Rotary Club meeting and he was set to be culture-vultured as the exotic afterthought. He was suspicious of the interview at first: 'Reminds me of talking to my old teacher – seein' the tape recorder there…' he fenced cagily. Once he settled in, Omar began exploiting the questions and was soon inspiring an audience grown up on the book. Omar had joined poetry at the hip-hop New Media slam juncture. The Don Bank audience, from being out of its comfort zone, embraced a rap style that grabbed you by the vitals as Omar's movement and delivery took on a mesmeric quality. Musa even offered up a Shakespearean sonnet.

As a convenor, this was one of most rewarding nights at LP ever, with two interviews and performances that had the audience entranced in two very different ways.

On the back of Tug's triumph from the month before, it was shaping to be a cracking year. That unmistakeable exhausted contentment (after telling oneself several times over the night, 'Just concentrate on the flow – breathe!') began to sink in on the drive home.

Anna Kerdijk Nicholson read 'Possession' in April – to another bounteous crowd!

I'd had a favour asked of me by Cathy Bray. A Janet Jackson was coming to Sydney from WA on some sort of national tour, was staying with Cathy, and wanted to know if she could be squeezed in at Don Bank in April. Anne's was a classy interview and the reading from her book sublimely enacted. You felt like a blank mind on Cook's voyage having details painted in by Anna's words.

In the interview, there was also a good analysis of what Australia Poetry had set out to do in the wake of the dissolution of the Poets Union, and so on; its ironic hopes for poetry's sustainability. The purveyors of poetry would be paying for it, not the public. The non-poets running AP needed to be informed adequately about the people embracing excellence and their ability to appreciate standards.

Janet Jackson was promoting her book *Q Finger*. Shambolic in interview responses (but giving a good sense of the Perth scene), she was a totally different person once she locked on to perform. The only poet we'd featured who physically touched a patron – a quick consoling hand on one man's shoulder during a piece more intimate than most. That put everyone on notice!

After supper, there was the launch of the Live Poets DVD of

the twentieth birthday party – with a special presentation made to the Stanton Library Local History Collection via Martin Ellis.

In the open section, a line from Randi (USA) was memorable: 'while you're looking for the loo you find this amazing view – at Woolhara'. Nashaa provided an English anecdote about the Arabic term '*Norumpta!*' (It remains). While rehearsing the latest APWG Sydney Writers Festival show, hearing that word was the sign for us all to pick up our suitcases! Robbie Westley did a song, 'I'll Ride This Vehicle'. It was her first visit to Don Bank and some homeless, priceless, eccentric part of the tradition was reaffirmed when we spontaneously applauded her irreverent offering.

May's Live Poets featured Clark Gormley, Cathy Bray and an unprompted surprise from the UK. The good crowds were almost a regular feature now. Clark Gormley from Newcastle revealed a lighter side of life – maybe! He performed his CD *Turn of Phrase*. Patrons got songs and poems in a funnybone romp here, Clark rounding off in 'A Cup of Tea', where a young damsel is invited to set down her woes by a Serial Killer in Simple Hippie's Clothing, dinky! At least that is how this convenor construed the too-good-to-be-true sentiment!

Then there was the irreverence of Cathy Bray. I felt I muffed her interview, had rehearsed the questions with her too many times maybe; the too-jokey references fell flat. Her lead piece, 'Mad Woman's Breakfast – Eat My Bush', a case of mooning George Dubya at the APEC summit, gives you some idea of the ongoing. And I used to think Cathy was such a sweet, harmless thing. We also got snatches of her latest Sydney Fringe Festival show, *A Poetree Growing Too Close to the House*.

Yet another something good – I finally persuaded Rima Najim (aka Soul Beats) to do a hip-hop number for us. That happened because of the night's third special guest arriving just before half-time. UK rapper Rich Bk had just been taken to dinner by a group of Rima's women friends, who then accompanied him to Don Bank. Rich lit us up with an irresistible sequence from his mobile phone, ending with a tribute to recently departed Gil Scott-Heron which was called 'The revolution WILL be Televised'.

In the open section, Jenni Nixon read 'City – neverending' which was cut from the last Harbour City Poets program. Sadly, she also had news of Kerry Leves' last days – to which I sang 'Song for Asking'. There was a lot going on. 'That was one of the best nights you've had!' Jenny Lee enthused meantime.

Billy Marshall Stoneking and Christina Conrads did a double act in June in 'Dialogue from the Edge'. Of a discontinuously dysfunctional association going back to Woodstock, that is. In a tribute to Billy, Paul Knoebel did 'Singing the Snake', an old favourite of Billy's, in the open section.

The feature was Bill MS and Christina's first reading together in seven years. 'Every time I see Stoneking after an absence, I feel so mad,' Christina said. 'That's just how the chemistry works. But he puts it down to reactions – but they are so honest!' Billy put character and meat on the bones. He saw finished, settled work. She saw chaos and rawness – beginnings with dark, unknown destinations. She was Spanish – the *duende* behind the black curtain: 'I have no history. To tell background, to embellish, is not my schtick! I'm just some possessed woman who's given up everything for her art. Creativity has nothing to do with intelligence.' She was a tedious, catalytic figure. Her perceptions saw words as different shapes and colours in the air. 'They lied about the words,' she said. 'You're always fighting the establishment of meaning. You can see all the words but not what they mean. That was Billy.' Any interview was superfluous. Christina made statements. Billy replied with poems linked by anecdote. Their interplay was intriguing – were they arguing or just doing the play so well? Did it matter? They went over time of course. We were hooked.

The second half presented a different joy. People read out literary letters – writers talking about writers, generally another writer they both hated! Danny read Chekhov about Tolstoy, Lamb about Byron, Kipling about Flaubert. Jenni Nixon read Katherine Mansfield on Shaw and Rebecca West on escaping the intentions of H.G. Wells! Bill T read Percy Shelley on Wordsworth and the poem 'Child Harolde'. Tami Sussman read Charlotte Bronte on Jane Austen. The audience was left howling! Letters Between Writers was a hit! 'We could do a stage play of these!' Billy M S enthused. Talk about this continued as Helen and I tried to clear up around people. Didn't they have homes to go to? This year was cracking along.

In July the special guest line-up read David Reiter and Jane Williams and the PR leaflet sported a picture of Joanne Featherstone with the provocative statement 'Poetry is Not a Choice!' She meant poetry was the only medium the director of the Red Room Company could choose to express herself. We were looking forward to her performance. But what do you do when one of your special guests does not show? It has only happened twice before at Don Bank from memory. The second time, the poet in question proceeded to jump into his car as soon as he was phoned. But I didn't have Jo's contact numbers. I kept changing the program hoping she would come through the door. Her no-show left the feature in the hands of Interactive Press.

David Reiter took us on a small tour of his latest work showing an online version as well as some live versifying. Some young ladies – recent regulars to Live Poets – were watching DR intently on how he handled an audience, mentally taking notes for their future stepping-out.

Tasmanian Jane Williams, a recent addition to Interactive's stable, struggled manfully with a cold in a small reading from *City of Possibilities* and had to cry off an interview.

A few nights before, a Geoff rang me to offer a banjo recital for Don Bank. We opened the second set with his jolly playing – uplifting a mixed night. Paul Knoebel offered a plea for sanity at the State Library abandoning its charter and selling off its book stocks to meet budget cuts – what will become of our civilisation without a book repository?

There had to be a comic interlude. When David Falcon began a poem by Robert Pinsky, he said, 'Unusually, it starts with "or".' Bob Howe cracked, 'There are three possibilities. There is Or. Or Awe. Or, why is it Awe? At least it wasn't awesome!' The audience groaned. Then Bill T hadn't brought any poems but I said, 'Why not read your poem "God and Truth" from *Light on Don Bank*?' Bill sat and squinted at the text. 'The print in this book keeps getting smaller!'

August was a music feature month with Cecilia Vilardo from Uruguay backed by Gilmar Munoz's guitar. A set of fado tempests underpinned the guitar's alchemical tapestry in a set of soul-capture. People were transfixed by Cecilia's heartbreaking tone – yearning, yearning! This was concert-quality stuff. As we went to supper, we were still absorbing it.

After the break, David Falcon – having to recreate some atmo – fought back with several fine poems, like his epic of a rower on the Murray and a requiem for the heroes who built the Sydney Harbour Bridge. Where Henri Mallard originally took the pics of the Bridge being built, Falcon had written the words. This poem would have been perfect for Martin Langford's book of Harbour City poems from Puncher and Wattman. Phil Radmall and Ava Banerjee – totally independently – presented poems centred on Brazilian culture.

September Live Poets was time for Bill Tibben to Reheat the Beats. Raw saxophone contrapuntals greeted the stroller-in under pictures of Parker C and Co blowing be-bop something bad in a smoky NY bar! Ginsburg and Kerouac later crackled on the night air – their images screened onto the wall from Bill's laptop. Corso was also there of course and Lawrence Ferlinghetti (who is still very much alive in San Fran).

Bill then offered a potted history of Beat Poetry and afterwards Bob Howe, David Falcon, Phil Radmall and this convenor all did beat poems or poems inspired by same. Falcon did an eye-opening backing to 'Kentucky Suite' by Philip Glass – the song/poem evocative of the American Plains orchestrating people's consciousness. Spoken Word of course owed a huge debt to the Beats.

After supper, Randall Stephens was Back from Borneo to wreathe the North Sydney jungle with road tales, like that about a performance poetry workshop in Kuala Lumpur. Stephens spoke also of a new venue in Melbourne – Sweet-Talkers – which is now on the same Wednesday of the month as Seven Towers Wednesday (Dublin) and Brooklyn's The Twisted Pepper, and Don Bank of course. 'But how weird is it?' Randall was asked. What sort of dynamic does it engender – arguing on Facebook?

In October, Polish-born Ludwika Amber delighted us with poems from *Our Territory*. Sometimes her sad tone indicated disquiet/mystery where there wasn't so much in the original language. Is 'Dolphins' not about the children we have who swim too far out? So far, we can only look on and hope for the best for them – until they take their place in the parchment of the sky. And what about the irony of her 'Old Black Woman', who is a girl again and no longer needs her breasts. An angel whose wings had disappeared. Ludwika's bottom line to me was 'We Slavs live through our literature to help life's problems.'

Ross Donlon, our other guest – from Melbourne – was Mr Understatement. Even bashful under questioning. 'This seems a good run I'm having now but you never take anything for granted.'

Ross (on rejections). 'It starts with the well-meaning and hastily written note ('No space this time!'). You know you've really made it when you graduate to the stamp – meaning not "thank you for your interest" but "piss off!"' But Ross wanted to know, 'How does the stamp know it is approaching a page from John Kinsella [the most published poet in the Australian universe]?' Ross on love: sixty-year-olds who are children again when they slip under the sheets – and 'the skin of her clitoris licks my thigh'.' On acceptance: 'Oh to be published in the *Easterly*, the *Southerly*, the *Westerly*, the *Northerly* and *Meanjin* – is it really only Aboriginal for "rejected by the *New Yorker*?"' (That last is actually originally from Frank Moorhouse.) There was Ross too trying to remember the shape of his father in the 'Old Blue Dressing Gown' (loved – with reason – by Bruce Dawe). So often you got the gag only a microsecond after Ross had intoned it. My personal favourite piece was 'Man with Moisturiser' (nuff said!), and a little troubling, I have to say!

In the open section, Amory Hill came back from heaven as 'Little Jack Horner'. Jenni Nixon's 'Eternity' was the story behind the man (Arthur Stace) behind the icon painted on Sydney streets. Danny Lockhart read a chilling 'Come into the Garden, Mary' from Kyla Ward.

A book I featured in the second half was Penguin's *Post-War Polish Poetry*. The standout was 'The Rain' and the poem that said, 'beware the spider that ties up the hands of a clock'. Bob Howe was genuinely effected by some of those gems.

November 2011: Carol Jenkins and another guest from Melbourne, Chris Wallace Crabbe. The fit of this program arose from a discussion with Chris Wallace-Crabbe at an Australian Poetry launch in March. Link Chris (the doyen of Australian literature) with one of his publishers: local poetry entrepreneur (River Road Press) and no mean practitioner herself – Carol Jenkins, author of 'Fishing in the Devonian'. Chris was the consummate pro in interview, performance and on the page. He had the hard-won nous to answer just enough: to concise an interviewer's questions complete. He then read from his books *Hawk from a Hand-saw* and *Domestic Sublime*. The poems: 'Surface of Things', 'Saucer', 'Indoor Yachting' (applying a 'fitted' bedsheet!), 'Coat Hangars', Garlic', 'At the Clothesline' – thence 'Delivering Tact', 'Speech of Birds', 'Summons in a Peak Period', 'Loving in Truth' and 'We are All Grown-ups'. He made of 'Sublime' simultaneously lofty heights and no-nonsense.

Carol's 'love of the craft', of 'seeing with words' – even to the infamous series of 'fridges she opened' in a laboratory – was manifest. I had been worried by her sometimes frail delivery at her launch at the Mosman Art Gallery. Here, people were lapping up her dextrous humour.

It was another big crowd and a monster open section: Chris Raft, 'Love in a Bar'; David Wansbrough, 'The Soup Warms Hearts'; two new poems from Ben Hession; Amory Hill, 'Talking to Canaries'; Shafic Ataya, 'This is how the world ends'; Bill Tibben, 'Ten things to put on my Fashion Mag Page'; Paul Giles, Blakean London Verses converted to 'Talking about Kardishan' (using text from a modern mag) and 'Nicole's Skin Therapy Cream'; David Falcon's 'Ode to a Rower'; Cecilia White, 'What was that? A fraction, a draft, a blank page – I have a headache!'; Cathy Bray, 'Daddy will you be home this time?'

There was more of Fadeel's flute from the reeds of the Marsh Arabs. This convenor finished with 'Yamba' – a poem/song take in homage to Salif Keita – at a key moment in a desert in Tanzania. Kelly from the council came – she's the new girl in charge of the cottage. We went out to maybe sing carols; instead we had a raffle in the courtyard. There were the annual UnDarwin Awards – how did we still finish relatively on time? Smart to have all the entertainment on before supper!

Found Poem, Cooma

How sweet it is to find a poem in the footpath
that doesn't begin and end with
Robbo, Shazza or Wazza Wuz Ere!
But there it was, etched with a conviction
to outweather decades:

SHANE ROCKS THE WORLD
AND ALL THE PRETTY GIRLS
CAN REST UPON THE KNEE OF JESUS

Enigmatic, evocative,
demanding to be puzzled at:
who was the Shane
who so boldly carved this barbaric yawp
in the concrete of a Cooma Street?
And what of the pretty girls?
Did they, or one of their kind, spurn him?
Did Christ press a better case?

Might these be the words of a modern-day Marvell?
One who, having spent his rhetorical stocks
failing to coax from his coy mistress
the jewel of her chastity,
was now washing his hands
of the whole gang of pretty girls
saving themselves for the Saviour?

SHANE ROCKS THE WORLD
AND ALL THE PRETTY GIRLS
CAN REST UPON THE KNEE OF JESUS

Jesus, that knee!
Not in the Lord's arms or bosom will all the pretty girls be blessed,
but 'rest upon the knee of Jesus' –
oh, lexical tease to tax the best!

*

It had been a bleak day, Shane –
a six-hour drive from Sydney,
hungover and hunted by murderous semis,
clocking the monotonous mounds of roadkill
I was trying not to become.

I checked in, the lone guest of a lonely motel,
and took a walk through the Alpine dusk,
armed with a bottle of rough red
in defence against the cold and my own company.
I sought the church where my mother,
the minister's daughter, grew up.

Maybe I was looking for something of myself
in the impossible gap of years,
in the melancholy proximity to my flesh's distant past.

I found neither church nor trace of my mother.
But along an empty stretch of road, between town and motel,
I did find your poem, Shane, a little epiphany of sorts:

SHANE ROCKS THE WORLD
AND ALL THE PRETTY GIRLS
CAN REST UPON THE KNEE OF JESUS

I studied the words in the fading light,
trying to riddle out the narrative
of you, the pretty girls and Jesus,
but at best could only second-guess.

Yet, I can't say why, you lent me a spark.
In years to come your blazon will remain,
testament to a man of fire and heart.
Decades hence others may stop and wonder,
ponder your puzzle with conjecture and rumour:
who was this Shane who rocked the world,
enigmatic street scribe of Cooma?

Tug Dumbly

Sacrifice

Grandma said
Ashes from incense
Make the finest talc
Perfect for suffocation

There is the river –
But a woman must do it
In that big bronze basin
In front of the family altar
Those tablets carved with
Names of male ancestors
And that thick register
Of male births

These things bear witness
To a woman's burden
Her guilt of bearing
A worthless
girl.

Mary Tang

The Fear

It was said,
'be afraid.'

And the people became afraid.

I stood
a dwarf in a petrified forest,
watching them dance the ancient dance –
there seemed joy in their terror,
laughter, too.

People baked bullets into their bread.
They chopped up newspapers
fried them
with sliced onions & sizzling steaks.
They stroked surveillance cameras
between their legs.
They treated TV screens like wells,
dipping buckets into them,
filling teacups
& offering them to neighbours.

At times it held the shape of mirrors & men,
but mostly,
the fear spread across the waking earth
as if it was a gas.

& gas expands to fill
whatever vessel
it is put in –

Today,
a man would not serve me at the supermarket.
A woman crossed the street to avoid me.
An anonymous email wished death upon me.

I, too,
became afraid.

Omar Musa

A Revolution: Televised

A revolution is being televised
in highly defined real time
where glass ceilings are now glass screens,
a touch responsive seat at the round table

where the disengaged, disenfranchised and dismissed
relax fists, unfurl fingers, flex thumbs
and press their own buttons,
breaking the Queen's English down to text speak.

This is the new norm.

Typed by apple consuming androids
downing tablets, pulling at crack berries and popping e-mails
at fibre optic superspeed,
curating unabridged masterpieces
because their lives are not being televised accurately.

Pixelated messenger pigeons tweet their truths
and wiki-leak their news from a bird's eye view,
because the revolution is powered by you!

Generation Wii!

Uber-connected multi-screen shottas
moving with the digitally displayed times,
scrolling with a contact list with thousands of online friends.
Ready to opt out, log off and spark new trends.

The revolution is pressure in groups,
challenging old regimes with sharp-witted memes,
exposing the emperor's new schemes
to plug in, turn on and co-opt their dreams.

This revolution is democratics for the demographic
cyber-dialled by the demographic,
bypassing established trenches,
questioning non-transparent firewalls…springs and falls,

because power is information
uploaded from covertly held phones,
infiltrating private parties or out on road
dropped in boxes marked 'to be told'.

The revolution is the hard drive of any man,
tirelessly hammering away at tomorrow
on a quest for release from the status quo,
scanning barcodes,
comparing meerkats to get the true facts
before he separates with his hard-earned cash for advertised fiction.

This is conventional science's friction –
those who wield insight, influence, buying-power
& snap their chatter in coded insta-grammar losing the Queen's diction.

The revolution is rubbing technology and tradition's quiet corridors
the right or wrong way, choose your sway –
bring on a new day.

Go wireless and cut your strings.
Copy your whims,
paste, forward and televise your revolution!

Tell them you're quietly brilliant and free to roam
on your own two feet.
The revolution means putting yourself in the driving seat.

Rich Blk

The Dig Tree

excerpt from 'The Factitious Tragedy of Burke & Wills, a poetic narrative'

Sitting in a veil and goggles against the flies
Wills writes *Dear Father, Cooper Creek is like*
and names an English stream. Looks at rat gnaw marks
on his belt, saddle, even his drawers,
and says aloud *But quite unlike.*

Gray looks up, grunts, gives a rattish grin,
as if to say *First sign o' madness, Mr Wills*
and Wills wonders, watching a sudden chase of galahs
in theatrical pinks and greys, *how in hell will this letter get…*
then corrects himself. *This letter
will get sent.*

*

In the increasing heat, all stalk around, chewing
whiskers or lips: supplies will not hold without Wright.

Christmas approaches, the choice is stay or go;
either way they need Menindee stores.

Menindee: the name alone drives
spontaneous 'ahhhs' from explorers who recall

Paine's Hotel, Captain Cadell's store, the ale,
and Mrs Paine

who was not niggardly in exposing
her arms. And was known, occasionally,

to show a foot, when rushing
from kitchen to inn.

*

But that was then:
since, tracks at Bulloo Lakes,
wheel marks, a horse's print.
Everyone had thought
(and Burke had said)
It's long-lost Leichhardt.

And everyone thought
*Poor bastard,
there but for the Grace of God…*
And everyone borrowed everyone else's copies
of early explorers and pencilled-in the risks.

*

After four months at Cooper Creek,
one is nearly dead, the rest have scurvy
and Brahe pats grit over a pit of supplies,
a note in a flask, and watches score marks
ooze sap. They retreat. Wright has not shown up.

*

Burke, King and Wills
walk into Cooper Creek.
Their camels collapse.
Wills sees a sign 'DIG
3FT N.W. APR 21 1861'. King and Wills
dig down, smash open the flask,
shout *They left today*,
they left today and all three
read the note. Burke murmurs
with six camels. Wills says *twelve horses*
and King adds *and ours are done in*.
They take the stores, rebury a note and leave.

*

Ten days later, Wright and Brahe ride in:
they kick around the camp and Wright says
Looks like there's been blacks about.

Brahe, who knows that Wright can't read,
says *Um, yes* but – no longer in command –
refrains from suggesting they dig.

After half an hour, Wright says *Let's leave*.

*

Three weeks after that, Wills – starving now –
walks back into camp. His face and feet are
blistered. He hunkers down to dig.
He finds no sign from Wright and Brahe.
On his eight-day walk, he's continued his notes
the better to understand my plight. He rips out
a journal page – noticing how his hands shake –
and writes, *Both camels are dead and our provisions done.*
We try to live the best way we can, like the blacks,
but find it hard work. Send provisions and clothes.

*

Within a month,
Wills is dead
but as he's dying
       he writes
        (still taking his pulse
        like the doctor's son
       he is)
            I can only look out,
                  like Mr Micawber,
                        for something
                              to turn up.

Anna Kerdijk Nicholson

the moon on her setting arc

as I go past the half-built homes
back to my kitchen
at the end of my day
the moon's on her setting arc
finding a path down the sky

her face is jaundiced
by smog and the dust
of all these construction sites
building and building trying
to stave off some dragon
or other
some tide of people or water
they're generating
so much that my nose blocks trying
to keep it out and my eyes flood trying
to wash it away and when I look at the moon

she's only halfway down
her setting arc but already
she's orange and dull

for a moment I think
her face is a lovely
fireside colour
but then I remember

she's the moon!
the silvery moon!
the pale goddess moon!

and right now
she's not
a goddess
she's a woman

looking down at her feet
as she goes out of sight
at the end of her day

her face all oranged
with the dust of men

Jackson

A Spade By Any Other Name

He calls a spade a shovel
and he calls a shovel a digger
and he calls a digger an ANZAC
which is a biscuit, only bigger.

And he calls a tap a faucet
and he calls a force-it a break-in
and a break in transmission means there's been
a stop-work meeting taken.

And he calls a drongo a jerk
and he calls a jerk a yank
and he calls a yank a septic
which is a crappy kind of tank.

Yes he calls it how he sees it
as he says, he pulls no punches
but he calls his mother twice a day
and she makes him all his lunches.

Clark Gormley

Tiger

Tiger, time in clinic checked
in a private centre text:
was his wife reportedly
a golf addiction therapy?

Doesn't Woods confess that they
saved transgressions yesterday?
Has he left home to repair
women holed up by affair?

Has Woods' story? Has Woods' star
then crashed his marriage as his car?
And who confirmed his face was clean
Woods' wife, one; to Woods, 14?

Woods the legend, Woods the Dad,
will Woods want the world he had?
Woods the gossip, Woods to make
rumours more than health could take?

As the wedded bevy flew
purported treatment rooms for two:
was his wife the first to see
his things exposed as VIP?

Tiger time in clinic checked
in a private centre sex
was his wife reportedly
made golf addiction therapy?

Paul Giles

I Have Poems

I have poems that would rather sleep
with women than be written down,
poems that stumble round unmade rooms,
unwashed & unafraid – in search of tongues
that have no answers & don't pretend to,
that have no tips about what to do
in Fukushima, other than dance the night away –
poems with scars desire has touched
having spent themselves in the company of
the deaf, craving love and destruction
with equal breaths, between a gasping nakedness
that knows its place & the price you pay
for loving much & too unwisely.
I have poems that left home years ago
without so much as a phone call or a fax,
huddled in the eternity of a Tuscan train,
watching, unnoticed, as the visiting violinist
practises Brahms, dreaming as the carriage rocks,
her fingers dancing on the fretless case.

Billy Marshall Stoneking

Round flat tin

My mother never opened her door
to traveling salesmen
though she once opened her door
to a rawleigh's man
he told her
he had a special cleaner
that would rid her of fly poo
she would not let him
open his voluminous bag

I longed to possess a round, flat tin
of pink rawleigh's ointment
my mother said
rawleigh's men were rough

when the hindu man
pulled up outside in his van
my mother leapt up his portable steps

inside the van
his long knife
flashed
he cut open
a pink watermelon
his dark face
his white teeth
his scales
shook as he weighed
the heavy fruit
black seeds
spilled.

Christina Conrads

Brothers

today
i rode my bike
near the river
we'd known as kids
the houses hefted on stilts
in memory of the 50s floods
the tracks along the banks
as lonely as our empty house

i thought of something you said
as we chipped up to the eighth green
at cabramatta last week
we were near the creek
and you said
you couldn't understand
why they didn't clean it up
so people could put boats in and use it

your words I knew
hid heartache and memories
i saw again for a moment
rowboats for hire
kids dropping from a rope tied high in the trees
oars slapping in rowlocks as missing fathers
rowed their sunday families upstream

David L Falcon

Man and Moisturiser

My skin is drying –
I'm scaly as a pearly alligator.
But the woman in the pharmacy
is encouraging, even cheerful –
tells me I can use this lotion all over my body.
(Then she pauses, as something occurs to her.)

Back home,
I adopt the pose of every clown or actor
I've seen spread greasepaint over stubble,
or every woman I've watched
tilt a chin, furrow a tongue,
then roll an eye at a mirror
to better see a spread of skin
and the self inside the self.
And how pleasurable it is,
immersion in a lake of lavender,
how like reversion into childhood's
sun cream, zinc cream, ice cream.

I soothe and spread, fingers breaststroke,
easing years from the wake I've sailed.
Grinless Easter Island face slips by,
flaws soften and disappear,
my mistakes filled with moisturiser.
I touch and retouch inside the mirror,
until smoother than a Henry Moore man,
past is perfect – no angles, I am an angel again,
wings invisible as my history.

Ross Donlon

Australian Language Landscape

To Sneja Gunew and Richard Reisner

Somewhere between the big cities
Sydney and Melbourne I stop on my way
amongst the rocks and eucalypts dropping bark
A bird flies by   or two
staying around close by   enticed my man

In the herb book of words
I have more and more names of birds
and write in my first language
those gum trees   those rocks   those birds
that we observe each other
in motion in colour
and take note in the bush

And later – much later –
we will all of it (*all of it?*)   translate
into a second language   and for a second time try
to touch the long swing of bark rope
on the branch of Australian air
and for a second time
we will patiently discover under our fingers
on these same bulges and splits in rocks
new sounds and words in the landscape

Ludwika Amber

Ode to Coffee

for Dimitri M.

Bean of the under cup, morning starter,
Cash crop, red-coated civet bait, first date.
Cake's companion, Romeo to the cigarette's Juliette,
Red bull in the china shop of sleep.
Bo-Peep-eyer, Bach-analian canto berry,
Universal stainer, unfair trader.
Heartbeat accelerator, headache
giver, headache taker, piddle maker.
Political agitator, habit dictator, your mode:
percolated, filtered, pressed a carbon-dater.
Literary hot-spot generator, cocoa's cousin, caffeine
conduit, substrate of small talk and revolution.
Retailer of the milk moustache, soy-latte decaf bypass,
picker-upper and putter-downer.
Machiavellian dehydrator, global drug of choice,
Bean that launched a million shops.

Carol Jenkins

Garlic

Adhesive, papery,
the wan delicate skin
sticks for just a smidgen
too long until

a naked clove
comes out successfully
shining
virginal as the dawn

yet leaving
its ripe sex on your fingers
for quite some time.

Christopher Wallace-Crabbe

LIVE POETS AT
DON BANK

4TH WEDNESDAY OF EVERY MONTH (FEBRUARY – NOVEMBER)

6 NAPIER STREET, NORTH SYDNEY

$7 Admission; includes supper and liquid refreshment
7.30pm – 10.30pm

INQUIRIES: (02) 9896 6936 or 0422263373 (mobile)
donnylivepoets@yahoo.com

All welcome to recite, sing, tell a story, play an instrument or just listen, if you'd like to!

WEDNESDAY JULY 25th

KATE MIDDLETON Sydney's (first) City Poet will talk about her role and read from her work.

KEVIN CLARKE will perform songs from his *Age of Irony* project and other material from his often edgy ouvre

LIVE POETS SUPPORTS REFUGEES

2012

Russia was the thread in our first Live Poets evening in February. Nora Krouk, a veteran of the local poetry scene, was born in Harbin, China, to a Jewish mother and a Russian father. She came to Australia in 1975 and has written poetry in Russian and English for decades. In interview, she talked about her early life in China, her journalism in Hong Kong, her enduring inspirations, the loss of her husband after so many years marriage. And the use of conversation in her poems. Was there a formula for her compositions? 'Does anyone really know the ending before you write a poem?' she asked. First memory vs the time machine. 'What makes memory come again and not be the same?' Nora read particularly from her latest book, *Warming to the Core of Things*.

The irrepressible David Wansbrough, who visits Moscow at least once a year through his Russian university connections and has introduced audiences there to several Australian poets, held the stage in the second half with poems from his latest book, *Le Pain Quotidien – poems on the pleasures of life*. The interview became a series of anecdotes – in Russia, about Russia and freedom, the characters David met. Regarding his other art – painting – 'What we don't "see" – that's why we paint, we have no words for how colour invests form.'

In the open section, Bill Tibben read 'Suburban Veneer' (penned on a trip to Broken Hill last year), while Ava Banerjee did a tribute to Whitney Houston.

Sheng Tong, who prepares a monthly anthology called *International Chinese Language and Literature Forum* in Chinese and English, was on his first visit to Live Poets and commented, 'If there was a meeting like this in China, the open section would be a competition and there'd be people walking out arguing at the end of the night.' Later, Sheng announced there should be the best open section poems at Live Poets each month in his anthology. It would start in July. I selected works from Ben Hession, Susan Adams, Jenni Nixon and David Falcon – along with some poems of mine, as Sheng Tong insisted. It was an encouraging start to the year in many respects.

We would get away from the book in March when Candy Royalle and Hameed Attai featured. There was no Helen and no hot supper. Delightedly, I greeted Jamal and Mohsen – for the first time in ages. 'We are just here to watch.' Jamal said with a smile.

Spoken word performer Candy Royalle, fresh from the Adelaide Fringe Festival, sang/read items from her *Stories by Starlight* show. Later that year, she was to win the Nimbin Poetry Cup – emulating her mentor, Tug Dumbly. Candy was initially inspired by Tug and Benito di Fonzo when they ran Bardflys at the Friend in Hand pub, Glebe, as she related in her interview. 'I've been doing different things with different media and persuasions but I always try to bring it back to poetry. At my shows the demographic is between seventeen and seventy! Hopefully I can present something they can all relate to.' She had chastised me for using a pretty image of her on the PR leaflet – defiantly gay, glamour wasn't her schtick any more! 'I'm trying to make a living out of this – I'm all about the feelings in the words. Giving the audience an unforgettable experience.' She told a story about recent work with a photographer. 'Imagine it – my words on the bodies of other people.' Like Omar the year before, she succeeded in rising above the Live Poets crowd's expectations of her.

In the second half, Hameed Attai sent a shiver down the spine with his songs of worship in Arabic. When interviewed, he declined to call himself a mosque singer and later showed his

Guy Sebastian side with some infectious pop tune a cappella. 'In English especially I sound like a girl.' His range means he's someone to watch in the future.

As a promotion for the Picasso exhibition at the Art Gallery of NSW, three patrons in the raffle draw had to pick which poem was written by Picasso from three pieces of verse proffered by the convenor. As it happened, Lou Steer, Ben Hession and Cathy Bray all picked the same poem as Picasso's! They were all correct and no one could get the prize!

While we were clearing up at the end of the night, Bob and I discussed Picasso's work. 'There's such a range to them – you can't like them all,' we agreed.

A Chinese lady, Miyah, won the wine in the raffle and said she heard about Live Poets via Ken Bock's announcements on 2RPH, radio for the print handicapped.

April saw an evening from the Kate Maclurcan songbook. Her contacts from the folk and choir world were there in force. The set included Eric Bogle's 'The Band Played Waltzing Matilda' and a moving tribute to Kate's father's time in the forces. In interview, she discussed what turns a person on 'to being part of a choir'. I told Kate I'd done the 'Grave' by Don Maclean a cappella before, knew it was a favourite of hers and maybe we could do it together – my vocal and her guitar. She elected to do the song on her own and dedicated it to me.

Guitarist Kevin Clarke came to Live Poets for the first time and Jim Low also did a few tunes. Poems from *Light on Don Bank* were read to honour the venue's birthday. Angela Fabie read a passionate piece behind her enthusiasm for the spoken word – this thing was catching! Angela and a uni friend of hers scored a lift from us several times back to Ermington.

The thrust of Jenni Nixon's feature in May, 'The Sydney Suite', centred on the city as an urban street collage. Think union green bans in Wooloomooloo. Think anti-Vietnam war marches. Think Arthur Stace's 'Eternity' painted over and over on the pavement. Also, several personal reflections interwoven classically with 'overheard conversations' were given theatrical emphasis. This trait can be sheeted back to Jenny's early work in repertory under the tutelage of Doris Fitton at the Independent a few streets away – subjects Jenny graphically revisited in interview.

There was a smallish crowd; the SWF climax followed quickly on our meeting's heels.

Since April, Live Poets had received a couple of invitations. One, to go to Waterloo Library to do a reading on National Poetry Day, the first Saturday in September. The other, to do a performance at Mosman Library in a Monday Matters session. Relatedly, there was later a spectacular end to Auburn Poets and Writers Group's performance at the Sydney Writers Festival. Proceedings started in an orderly enough fashion from a Bedouin tent at Railway Park, Auburn. But when the generator failed, the lights went out. APWG had to declaim amongst a by then considerable crowd, backlit by car headlights from some cooperative patrons! This was interaction at a new level!

June Live Poets saw a long-held ambition realised – securing a visit from Rhyll McMaster. Rhyll's interview intrigued with discussion of her ambitions to be a farmer and how, in a reversal of the usual way things worked, she turned some lines of her poetry into the novel which became the award-winning *Feather Man*. Afterwards Rhyll took us all late-night shopping (with Charles Darwin and Ned Kelly in her trolley) through the pages of her latest book.

David Musgrave featured in the second half. He was in the form of his writing life and about to clinch his second Newcastle Prize for poetry. But he vividly relived in interview the onset of depression which overshadowed his winning the prestigious Newcastle on the first occasion. He read from 'Concrete Tuesday' and other newer work.

In the open section, Mike Richter performed a shanty, 'Tall Ship and Up-Chuck!', and first-timer Abigail played her harp. Realising there had been a dearth of music this night, Bill Tibben and this convenor closed proceedings with an a cappella rendition of Chain's early-1970s hit 'Black and Blue'.

Kate Middleton – not the one who married a prince but the lass appointed as Sydney's first City Poet – was the poetry special guest in July. She was influenced by the American countryside considerably during her studies at the University of Michigan – there was a long segmented journey down the Colorado river in her latest book, *Ephemeral Waters*. But it was just as much about emotion filtered through a sensibility. Kate in interview filled us in on what being a City Poet entailed.

When Canadian Kevin Clarke first came to Live Poets a couple of months before, I mentally earmarked him as a future music guest. Five hit-worthy songs – all but one his own compositions – confirmed that intuition this night. He even got us to sing along on three tunes. Kevin both spoke and sung about his teenagehood in a family of budding singer-songwriters and how going punk at a university party threatened to typecast him. One song was the soundtrack to a video about Lavender Bay entered in the Vivid City competition. It made the shortlist.

Another musical regular, Lee Cass, was moving home and brought in a slew of books for raffling later. David Wansbrough meantime read two psalms from his libretto about brilliant young concert pianist Aaron Macmillan, who'd recently discovered he has a brain tumour. Ian Bryce also turned up after a long absence and discussed with Lee Cass and myself over a red wine how we should show poetry's more humorous side. Lee had an idea for a night of Bawdy Verse – 'Tales from a Bawdello!' say. Ian, after two years' conversation with my Don Bank email updates, surfaced virtually bulging with clever rhymes.

Skye Loneragan – our special guest in August – is regarded by many as the premier spoken word exponent in Australia and she did not disappoint. She was so 'on', her interview became part of her performance and vice versa. She exhibited a dizzying array of emotions and characters in diverse situations in a forty-minute display with no recourse to notes.

This evening also saw the release of the latest edition of the aforementioned *International Chinese Language and Literature Forum* quarterly. It featured five Live Poets regulars with poems chosen from the open section over the previous six months. They each read their poem out to the audience. Jenni Nixon had the thrill of hearing her poem 'Missing' also read out in Chinese by editor Sheng Tong.

The 18th Sydney Biennale, entitled All Our Relations, was discussed in the context of the question 'Where is Art today with its role as the boundary-breaker largely superseded by terrorism, and concerns about the environment?'

Among the open section readers, Rose Naughton spoke of the 'the unloved body of a Bondi tramp' and Bill Tibben read the 'Pleiades (Star Cycle)'.

September's Language is Our Business in recognition of the Year of Reading provided something out of the box. Arguably inspired by the London Games, Live Poets presented the Literature Olympics.

Everyone was invited to bring along their choice of the finest writing – from any genre and from any time in recorded history. It could be a nursery rhyme, a fairy tale, a limerick, a myth or fable, a song lyric, a short story, a play monologue, or a scene from a novel, a piece of journalism or a public speech – not to mention a poem! The only stipulation was that each piece presented could be no longer than three minutes.

Any people who hadn't brought along their favourite piece could inhabit what this convenor had on hand to read out. With an eye to various bedtimes, the Games started with a scene from Doctor Seuss's *Cat in the Hat* and a physical acting out of various nursery rhymes by City of Sydney Children and Young Adults Librarian Beth Koorey and her ukulele. We ended with Molly Bloom's bawdy soliloquy from James Joyce's novel *Ulysses* re-enacted by the inimitable Marie McMillan. This night proved so popular, several people want it be the Olympics every year at Don Bank!

For the pernickety-minded, the following is a list of who presented what. 1 Marie McMillan (*Cat in the Hat*). 2 Beth Koorey (physical nursery rhymes – with ukulele and hand gestures). 3 Michael Barfield (Wicked Kids story from Paul Jennings/Maurice Gleitzman's book). 4 Bill Tibben and Rosemary Naughton ('Jabberwocky' and 'Owl and the Pussycat'). 5 Frank the Poet Ebzury ('May I Feel?' by ee cummings). 6 Peter Wagner (Ogden Nash, various limericks). 7 Cathy Bray (a couple of Aesop's Fables). 8 Danny ('Johnny and the Leather Bottle' by Italo Calvino) and 9 When Death Came (Tiwi creation myth). 10 Lou Steer (a ghost story). 11 Amory Hill (the poem 'Bus to Bihaj'). 12 George Clarke and partner ('Highwayman Comes Riding' and a David Malouf poem). 13 Dianne Schultz Tesmar ('Catholic Priest' by Talbot McCarroll). 14 Cathy Bray (a Les Murray poem). 15 Danny ('Telephone Conversation' by African immigrant poet Wole Soyinka, seeking accommodation in the UK). 16 Kerrie Jamieson read – what? 17 Vicki McDonald (a long poem by A.E. Housman). 18 George Clarke (speech from *Henry V* by Shakespeare). 19 Jenni Nixon (from *Taming of the Shrew* by Shakespeare). 20 Peter Wagner (from *Hamlet* by

Shakespeare). 21 Jenni Nixon (a Vicki Viidikas poem). 22 Barvara Hush (passage from *Cider With Rosie* by Laurie Lee). 23 Danny G (Martin Luther King speech). 24 Lou Steer (Queen Elizabeth I addressing the people on the eve of the coming of the Spanish Armada). 25 Rosemary Naughton (insults from various writers). 26 More Aesop's Fables – but who read them? Marie McMillan (Molly Bloom soliloquy from James Joyce's *Ulysses*).

One final note here: this convenor rather sprung the Bloom piece cold on Marie feeling she would relish throwing the text on as is, in character – like growing into a lascivious negligée. But after some consternation she went off into a corner as the first half rolled on and began furiously making adjustments to the photocopied pages. I imagined she was identifying then removing all the cuss words from Molly's/Joyce's mind. But no. She was in fact punctuating the piece. (Joyce was famous for eschewing this detail!) 'Without the full stops and the commas, I wouldn't know when to pause and/or emphasise!' Marie explained in a voice that reminded one of Helen Mirren.

Come October and it was time to welcome Crow's Nest's Ed Wilson and the South Coast's Chris Mansell. Ed was having his latest *Collected* launched by Kardoorair Press boss Anthony Bennett. He also talked about how his poetry cross-references with the painting he's taken up since his retirement from his job at the Royal Botanic Gardens.

Chris Mansell, originator and director of the Shoalhaven Writers Festival for several years, regaled the audience with anecdotes about the above and her formation of Press Press chapbook publishing – before her intimate, lively, at times sensuous reading. Bennett then launched Ed's book. It represented fifty years of Wilson's writing: 'It's my silver anniversary!' he quipped.

Several other Kardoorair authors, like Tony Scanlon, Bill

Tibben, John Carey – Chris Mansell has also appeared under its imprint – were in the audience. The generous supply of Poet's Corner wine and a selection of gourmet sandwiches augmented the festivities in the courtyard.

So much so the night's second half became a swapping of poems and reminisces around the campfire – the exchange including past Live Poets guest/artist Richard Tipping. I only lamented the fact I was still ill from a bout of flu that had ruined a recent journalistic assignment in Surfers Paradise – red wine doesn't mix well with antibiotics.

November's Live Poets had a steam-punk theme (first guest Lou Steer had appeared in the local paper the week before with wires coming out of her head!). With backing by creative bassist Elsen 'Paisty' Price, Lou presented 'Wild Red Heart', a sequence that teetered into burlesque at times. Husband Brian Martin did a video of Lou's rather outré performance which was the buzz of the courtyard supper conversation.

But the night was not even half over. Even without the non-appearance of fabled import from France, Stephen Morris, who apparently couldn't get a visa!

Local 'bard with bongos' Benito di Fonzo (accused of being a performanceholic in his interview – he retorted he was a playwright not a performer) rib-tickled aplenty with his wry, neo-beat, louche lounge-lizard style. His revisit of volunteers' advice to Sydney Olympics tourists was a howler.

The reaction to the cameo appearance of Freddy Lyman to open and farewell the cocktail hour – with his songs 'Goody Goody' and 'Why do Fools Fall in Love?' respectively – was largely unrecorded as we went to press. A roll-out of the vaunted UnDarwin Awards and a vignette from first-timer Chris Brimo (invited by Benito) sent us out into the night.

My Poems in Russian

deal with the past –
its joys and disasters
its yearnings and trust
a search for the core
for a spark (if any)
it drops with a clanger –
proverbial penny
and things are revealed
and it is too late
for building a castle
and cheating fate…

The cat tries to soothe me
with claws and purr
he has such a tomcatty
tiger fur!
He has no regrets
(this fortunate creature)
as I'm trying hard
to upgrade my nature.
Promise – no more
desperate poems!

Nora Krouk

The Ordinary Order of Things

Lovely is the clacking of knitters,
the chatter and clicking of needles,
the looping and hooking,
locking and linking its language:
hold your hands out as the skein
winds down to balls,
with knit one, purl one, drop one,
cast one, slip one.
Stories and wool are yarns.
And grandmas' gossiping banter
as rheumatic fingers think
through knitting needles
independent of the talk.
What wisdom is woven in patterns:
knitted chains twisted from the shoulder
to wrist and ribbed cuffs.
A boy's jumper will have
interlocking lemniscates
flowing down his spine.
Knit one, purl one, cast off the row.
In knitting life's threads flow.

Dig the earth and plant a word.
Sounds from the soil taste sweet on the tongue.
Sage, lovage, fennel,
borage, peppermint, dill,
lettuce, cabbage, basil,
onion and chives, parsley, spinach,
rose hips, nasturtiums, star anise,
cardamom, ginger, angelica,
caraway, marjoram, tarragon, coriander.
And thyme.
And the weather and the seasons,
the sun and the moon tides,
and the pregnant autumn.
And the tilling, dibbling, seed sowing,
waiting, weeding, plucking and eating.
All part of the dancing rhythm of life.

Near Solnechnogorsk at an outdoor table,
with frothy beer and crusty bread,
peasants gather around the great grande dame
of the village collective
(who in her day had bashed Germans).

Now she comforts a baby girl
who gums her knotty knuckle,
until a mother unbuttons
her full blouse and takes the child to suckle.
Little hands squeeze and knead the breast
and her tiny feet
pulsate against the palm
of mum's hand.
A kid digs spreading dust on feet
with a whittled toy spade.
'Soon,' chuckles great-gran.
And the aunties laugh
and the cosmos turns.
'Ah' outbreathes the world,
'men' inbreathes the earth.
'Amen.'
That is the way of it.
The dance. So be it.

David Wansbrough

Sea Heaver

I must heave over the lee rail again, to feed the fish, oh why,
When all I asked for was a still ship, in a dockyard high and dry.
And the swell's kick and the wind's song, just leaves my stomach aching,
With a sea-grey face as I chunder, producing technicolour retching.

We must move further from the seas again, for the 'hurr-rr-hhh' of a chunder
Is a wild call and a clear call, that may not be denied;
And all I beg for is a palm tree, for peaceful reclining,
Away from the flung lunch and the blown spew, and seagulls recycling.

So why should I go down to the seas again? To the retching, queasy life,
It's the gull's way and the whale's way, but for me it's painful strife;
So all I ask is to be upwind, from a liquid-laughing fellow-heaver
And a quiet sleep and a Stemetil, when the long chuck's over.

Mike Richter

Stealing Paradise

for Robert Adamson

It was true love at first sight…
The glossy black feathers, the splendid orange and green plumage,
the calm wise eyes of the bird of paradise painted by John Gould.
So gorgeous compared to the everyday birds he rescued – the cheeky
street kid sparrows and rats on wings called pigeons, fallen from
their nest too soon, barely feathered.
He nurtured them all in his backyard aviary but now, seeing this
exotic creature, he knew ambition.
The rainforests of New Guinea so far away from his city home,
He imagined them to be like the set of a Tarzan movie, he the lone
pith helmeted explorer paddling upriver to find the bird's home, in a
place where dark feet drummed the bare earth and where dark heads
wore those spectacular plumes in headdresses even more fanciful
than the bird itself.
Instead of living the drama of life, he was a miserable captive in
a dingy classroom, where the birds flew free outside the window,
while the words and numbers danced before him on the page, to
tumble into a heap of confusion and ignorance.
And then he found the prize – not in the dark forests – but only a
bus trip from home in the zoo owned by a rich man on the harbour.
He knew bolts and bars could not keep him and his bird apart.
They belonged to each other, each trapped in a cage made by other
people. Together, they could be free.
He waited until the day trippers left, then it was easy – a bolt-cutter,
a hessian bag. He took a few more beauties away for good measure.
When they saw him, they did not cry out or give him away. They
recognised their saviour.

He took them home and they kept company with the drab little city birds, until the day the police came (damn nosy neighbours). His mum loyally said, 'He finds all those birds in Cammeray Park.'

He soon found himself in a more secure cage, one far from his beauties and home. His jailers were raptors, but no more so than his fellow captives, who fought and squabbled over nothing.

He still dreamed of flight and found it in jacking fast cars, leading to more cages until they put him in the biggest most secure one of all – the Bay. The stone tomb built on a cliff edge where all the windows face inwards, away from the sea.

He longed to be an albatross, soaring forever over those wild blue waves, but instead, he cowered, a broken street kid sparrow, in his tiny cell.

Until the day he heard a different songbird, the leather clad joker to his thief. The words came pouring out of him at last, confused no longer, taking form and shape, sweet poetry.

The cage door swung open at last and he fled into the open arms of fear and desperate temptation. But the words kept flowing, no matter how often he sought oblivion in poppy dreams.

Now, after the tumult of a life lived for escape, he sits on the beach at Jerusalem Bay at his granddad's place, fishing for jewies while the words keep dancing in his head until they fall into shape on the page.

No need to steal paradise now, he lives it every day.

Lou Steer

Borderlines

1

forty-three West Papuan men women and children
five weeks in wild seas in a traditional double outrigger canoe
drifting four days without food or water
washed ashore on Queensland's Cape York Peninsula
relocated to Christmas Island – *if sent back we will die*
one of many who served prison time for raising outlawed flag
pro-independence activists for decades are hunted in the jungle
a slow genocide: raped   imprisoned   tortured   shot
bodies thrown in the river   houses burnt   land occupied
boys from the remote highlands – sent alone to the sea

while at the north-west point on Christmas Island
construction cranes swoop across a new detention centre
another prison for those who flee persecution

2

out-of-control bushfires burn red across the skyline
cricket bats *thwack*   tennis balls to racquet's *pock*
in scorching summer heat   frolic in a pool
dive in the ocean   who cares about refugees?

climate change is absolute crap says Tony Abbott
evacuees from drowned islands   homes swallowed by the sea
are economic migrants we deliver straight to PNG

the Australian navy tows asylum boats back
cuts them loose in Indonesian waters
            saves refugees from drowning
who surrender then to suicidal despair

seeking asylum is a human right – our colonial plan:
        dump 'em overseas
fails to meet international standards
the UN found conditions on Manus Island
harsh hot humid damp and cramped

3

next we must stop the birds
crossing sovereign borders
send them packing
process them in cages offshore
as the European pigeon said to an Indian mynah:
go back where you came from!

                                    Jenni Nixon

A Little Laugh I Lost Somewhere

It's in my back pocket!
Flattened, faded, folded
forgotten in the wash

No
it's in my top drawer
rattling around with ink-dry pens
I'm determined to use
gouging disbelieving circles
on an innocent page
till I throw them all back in a rage
rather than the rubbish

No
it's lying beneath the mattress
suffocating from neglect
half of it crushed under
half a depressed double bed

Or
it's boxed in
between shelved experience
in the closet
slowly growing hard

it's run away to the circus
it's lost in the pile
it's left between two cinema seats
watching credits cease to roll
above a darkened aisle

And
it's caught between the pages
of heavy, historical rift –
it's been blown to bits
out the window

It's got mixed up with all my money
folded thin between two notes.

It's hiding in the toy basket
it's given up
stroking your hair
this,
this:
a little laugh I lost somewhere.

Skye Loneragan

Heartland

My crumpled face, each line a poem,
veins in my arm, corky liane;
a brace of conscience from the farm –
young Peter will not make old bones.

This meteor has made his run,
with nose-cone of titanium;
and his re-entry burnt my heart,
who did not see the fuzzy star.

A Northern Star who fell from grace
while we still arbitrate and trade,
my father died at such an age;
now Halley hurtles into space.

And in the cold sieve of the night
we squint at the receding light
and of my three-score-year-and-ten –
I will not see this star again.

Ed Wilson

In April 1986 I had been looking through some old papers at the Lismore office of *The Northern Star* newspaper when I read of the death of Dr Peter den Exter, 'friend of the forest', after trying to control a burn-off at his Terania Creek property. He had died just before the return of Halley's Comet. We shared an overlapping geography and interest in orchids. I met him first at Terranorra, then later at the University of New England. *Vale* Peter den Exter.

On Shanghai Road

After the night markets, amber, smog-thick light
glowers over Shanghai Road. In doorways
on corners strewn with the market's debris
pale-faced ladies of the night are marooned
by morning, waiting still for customers.
Mainland girls, perhaps, from Guangdong towns
smile reflexively, the merest rictus of the mouth,
as I walk by, bored and aimless in the dawn.

Soon Mong Kok and Yau Ma Tei will teem
with Sunday's maids, free for the day from their toil
in cramped, decaying, high-rise apartments;
raucous Filipinas in too-tight jeans, teenage Javanese;
slim, giggling Sumatrans in brilliant head scarves.

The chattering maids with their mobile phones;
these sallow, silent girls clutching handbags,
ankle-deep in litter on Shanghai Road; and I –
all of us exiles here in these concrete canyons,
here through fate or indigence or choice,
hawking whatever it is we have to sell.

Anthony Scanlon

She Chucked a Sickie

She should've gone to work that day
but instead she chucked a sickie

and made a breakfast in bed
of the flowers of insolence
as she got sloshed as an alcoholic melancholic
on the ale of irresponsibility
in the back of the beer garden of Earthly delights.

She chucked a sickie,
and Capitalism didn't collapse
and the company that she worked for
sold just as much superfluous crap,

as she took a laissez-faire approach to the day
and lay like an unemployed concubine
on his street-find futon
wrapping the semi-soiled sheets of deep fried sins
around her like a sari.

She chucked a sickie
and the Australian Stock Exchange didn't fold in
upon it's own bloated sense of self-importance
as she swapped the saccharine
of her corporate workplace
for the royal jelly of licentious licence.

And the Dow Jones and Nikkei didn't even notice
as he lay nibbling at her nipples
like they were bonbonnieres at an ethnic wedding.

And Wall Street wasn't worried
when they segued their bodies
back into one another.

And, once again, analysts of the relationship
between interest rates and the Balance of Payments
completely failed to take into account
that they were marking midday
by lighting roll-your-own clichés in bed.

But she should've gone to work that day
and instead she chucked a sickie,
and loved it.

And the Free World, for whatever that means,
didn't fall into disrepair,

and nobody went blind,
and it didn't lead to heroin.

As a matter of fact
no other object in the universe,
aside from her boss,
seemed to notice her absence

and she realised
that tomorrow, if she wanted to,
she could just quit.

Benito Di Fonzo

Dear God

1

God made the world.
Then he woke up.

2

God called his analyst.
'I had this dream,' he said.
'I am listening,' she said,
'but I have to charge extra:
You know what day it is.'

3

God had to make the world twice.
The first time it was perfect.

4

God rang AAMI.
They said 'No cover for acts of God,'
afterwards relented, plumped up premium.

5

God made the world.
Then he wrapped it up, like Christo:
that's why we are in the dark.

He gave it away as a present
so we are here now.

6

God made a play The World.
They had it adapted for film.
They wouldn't let him direct.
They hired the hotshot whizz-kid
from downunder.

7

God wrote a poem.
He called it The Universe.

8

He had time on his hands
once he made the Universe.

9

God aspired to stand up.
He presented 'Life on Earth' at the festival.
The Critics sniffed, called it routine,
until without missing a beat
God ad libbed death.
They begged for an encore.
God sighed and incorporated reincarnation.
Some suspected it wasn't entirely original.

10

Little light music, dark open opus;
riddle riddled with contradiction;
play clay, lust dust, mad mud,
sky-in-the-pie, I of the day;
Novel novel, fusion fiction,
dream of consciousness;
imaginal installation.

God pondered his work.
Man, whose very being unravelled everything
ready-made.
But was it heart?

11

God made love.
The earth moved.

12

God didn't make the world for money.
He made it for free.

Ten Ch'in Ü

Poetry and Presenting it in Public Part Four

Can performance poetry be learnt?

Scott Sandwich: Sure it can! I can teach you everything I know right here. Step #1: just be yourself. For example, there is no difference between me onstage, or offstage, and I write the way I talk. I'm just some person, and I'm introducing myself…the poem I'm performing is something I'm sharing with you. All my favourite performers, comedians, writers…every time I see or hear them, I feel like I'm being invited to understand them, not just the things coming out of their mouths. That goes for everyone, by the way. Classical composers, vaudevillians, photographers, film-makers… Mysterious people don't really interest me. I like the ones who show me something.

David Falcon: I don't see a major difference between 'performance' and other poetry but there is a world of difference between a bad delivery and a good one. So I think in relation to performance, assuming the poetry generally is of a good standard, the learning focus needs to be on the delivery.

Phil Radmall: I think this is an inhibition thing. The best performance poets just have presence and pizzazz.

Susan Adams: Certainly performance poetry can be improved.

Willem Tibben: Do you mean writing or performing? Yes and yes as much as any other forms.

Richard James Allen: Rhythm and timing are key ingredients in performance poetry, which, ideally, are innate sensitivities, but can also be brought to consciousness, observed in others and honed as part of your skill set. When performance poetry began, there were no rules or guidelines. Ppoets were making things up as they went along. Now the form has evolved to have its own tropes, which makes it sometimes more predictable, but also more sophisticated. And therefore, like any form, more communicable.

Erwin Zehentner: If you are willing to go to acting courses and spend four or five years being a tree or a marsupial… Ever seen a tree read Goethe's 'Erlkoenig'? Awesome.

Cathy Bray: Performance can always be improved. However, a poem that was not written for performance cannot be tortured into life.

Edwin Wilson: Aspects of performance poetry can be learnt, but, once more, raw talent aspects cannot be taught. The personality of the poet can be a factor here, some of whom may be too introspective, and almost too sensitive to the memory of the emotional intensity of a particular poem to read the words aloud.

What do you when you realise your reading/performing poetry is not cutting through?

David Falcon: I think it is too late to do much about it at the time. The best thing is to learn from the experience and improve for next time.

Phil Radmall: Weep and move on. Otherwise, try something different, or use the experience to inform future attempts.

Paul Buckberry: Generally, I'll stick with the program and read or perform what I'd planned. Afterwards, I'll access what might have worked differently, poem choices, style, take audience and venue into consideration, was this my show or was I part of a show. All the findings would be funnelled into the next performance for hopefully a different result.

Erwin Zehentner: Finish off with a quick haiku. Don't forget a reference to a tough audience, which will make everyone feel superior as you slowly slink out through the cracks in the floorboards.

Willem Tibben: I used to stop. I tend to soldier on now. Very occasionally I have drawn attention during the reading to the lack of cut, as a ploy to get more attention. Sometimes it feels as if it isn't cutting but turns out that it was – or vice versa. That is, the audience's reaction is in part imagined, based on my own response to me reading as it is happening.

Benito di Fonzo: Drink up and get on with it… Or maybe change tack/material.

Les Wicks: It's very hard to turn the ship around in a small time bracket.

Kate Lilley: Act professionally and carry on.

Martin Langford: No one has an oeuvre in which they can find poems which would suit every audience. Adjust – but you can only do the best you can with the material you've got.

Richard James Allen: Stop. Breathe. Slow down. Speed up. Jump ahead. Check in with your audience. Improvise. Make a joke. Change the poem. Throw the spotlight to something else. Pick up afresh. Or exit stage left!

Cathy Bray: Stop. Stop punishing yourself and your audience. I want my audience to enjoy my poetry as much as I do – no cutting or pushing through. I'm performing poetry, not pyramid selling.

Candy Royalle: I test all my new work on a small audience before I take it to the big shows so that I know it's definitely going to connect. On those rare occasions where it doesn't, I just take it on board as a lesson learnt.

Susan Adams: Take advice from trusted sources – perhaps workshops. Be aware that if you are not enjoying the presentation/reading the audience won't be either. Practise, rehearse…

Edwin Wilson: It is probably best to say, this one is not working and to actually stop, and then finish up with something punchy and short and sharp, and preferably road-tested before. We've all 'been there done that' of course and can only learn by doing. Part of the trick is to match the poem with the audience, and poems read by other people on the night. At my first ever professional reading – in the Open Section of Poets at the Pub in Glebe – I'd recited my 'Nancy of the Afterglow', a parody of 'Clancy' road-tested some years before at an Australian Museum Christmas party, where people got all the in-jokes. This poem had been well received by the pub crowd. On the strength of that, I'd been invited by Patricia Laird – a mover in the poetry scene at the time – to read at another function. Because of my inexperience, I'd started off with my 'Nancy' poem, which completely bombed. The poem had been slightly rude – fine for a more raunchy pub or museum party environment, but not for this crowd, well-dressed, middle-class ethnic women, who had not been educated in the tradition of the Banjo as I had been at school, and would not have picked up on the literary references. So I changed tack, and went more French-symbolist, more intellectual and more upmarket and saved myself!

Scott Sandwich: Many of my poems have extra lines – or even paragraphs – that I only use when I feel like I've said something that an audience hasn't understood properly. There aren't many because after a few performances you know what works and what doesn't. My performances aren't static. Some of them are so conversational that I can change them as freely as the way I could rephrase something when talking to a friend. I also wave my arms a lot, but I can always flail more.

Is a poet's background, educational qualifications or sexual preferences important?

Candy Royalle: This is a strange question! I'm not sure what you mean. Is it important to know that stuff before hearing/reading their work? Absolutely not. Who cares? It's about whether the work is beautiful and connects. If their work is informed by their background or sexuality, then it is important to them in any case – important enough for them to write about it.

Susan Adams: All backgrounds and experiences are important – it's where we draw our emotional responses. I don't think academic qualifications are necessary to be able to write good poetry but they certainly help with the knowledge and understanding of the great writers before us.

Richard James Allen: Important? Yes and no. Yes, for what these things bring. No, for whether one thing is more cool, appropriate or worthy than any other.

Willem Tibben: Important for what? 'Q: Would I hit a woman with a child? A: No, I'd use a brick' is as good an answer as any to this question.

Martin Langford: Sadly, yes, in some cases. And much more subtly than just the obvious things, for example, age, accent, dress and so on. All potentially play a part.

Kate Lilley: Everything's important.

Benito di Fonzo: It's only important to them [the poet]. You use everything you have in your storytelling. So, if you can use it, good.

Edwin Wilson: They should not be important. People from different cultures can sometimes have an advantage in the Anglosphere, and stand out because of their difference. And poets in minority languages are often more treasured in their own cultures than poets who write in the English language.

Cathy Bray: It's important only in defining what they have to say in the poem – none of these factors alone is going to make them a great poet.

Erwin Zehentner: Don't bitch if you go to a gay bar and everyone talks about coming out… Similarly, when going to the royal society of poets you can expect to hear from highbrow readers – your four-line limericks may just not cut it.

David Falcon: Much more important is how sensitively and expressively we are able to draw on those. Every aspect of life and living can be grist for the mill of a good poet but no amount of richness will replace the skill and hard work which expresses it in a form which can strike a chord with the rest of humanity.

Paul Buckberry: Well, it's important to the poet because we are all be subtotal of our experiences, education and the like included. And a poet's background is sometimes important to select members of the audience. Often the latter is in a judgemental way.

Scott Sandwich: Important? Nope! I think these things can come out through the words, if they need to. The same way they're not important when you watch an actor, or a musician. If the audience needs to know, then they can find out. If you want people to know something about you, then tell them – just like meeting someone at a party. If your identity is important to that work, then your identity is already in it.

LIVE POETS AT

4TH WEDNESDAY OF EVERY MONTH (FEBRUARY – NOVEMBER)

6 NAPIER STREET, NORTH SYDNEY

$7 Admission includes supper and liquid refreshment
7.30pm – 10.30pm

INQUIRIES: (02) 9896 6956 or 0422263373 (mobile)
dannylivepoets@yahoo.com

All welcome to recite, sing, tell a story, play an instrument or just listen if you'd like to!

WEDNESDAY May 22nd

The joy and passion of
ANNA SALLEH
will present:
Songs of Brazil.

ASTROLOGY WRITES!
Poems inspired by the influence of the Stars Signs
with JULIA and DEREK PARKER

Open Section

LIVE POETS SUPPORTS REFUGEES

2013

February Live Poets was a hot night in more ways than one. The guests were Robert Adamson and Kate Lilley. People were making bookings a couple of weeks beforehand. The gate was the biggest for a non-birthday party milestone ever, outweighing the record numbers for Tug Dumbly and Michelle Cahill and Kate Waterhouse. We had trouble getting windows open, getting enough air into the place.

We began with nostalgia – the return of David Tribe and Craig Powell (with a walking stick, mind you) after ages away. Craig's poem about his father was sublime. Kate Lilley then came on and talked about the making of her groundbreaking book of poetry *Ladylike* and its method of generating aspects of the self – and Kate working on a collected edition of her famous mother Dorothy Hewett's poetry. High from talking, her reading then plumbed the emotions – a journey seemingly under the water of identity.

The scheduling of this evening – getting everything in – was tricky if everything went to plan. But after supper there was a problem. I abandoned the raffle because I sensed people just wanted to hear the poets. Bob had left to move his car, afraid he was in a no-park zone, and didn't come back. We waited. I decided to read a poem of mine and then my favourite one of Bob's – to bring about his return. We waited some more. The original parking spot was so far away – that was all. He re-emerged, everyone relaxed and we began the interview.

I had outlined to Robert a simple, precise plan. I would introduce a turning point in his long career and he would answer one question about it. It was never going to be that simple of course, and hilariously so. Robert was voluminous in his responses and associated anecdotes and sidebars (in journalistic parlance) stacked on each other. Eventually we had made a long journey through Bob's life – no one had left – and now there were the poems he wanted to read. And Robert always delighted in immersion in his work – with more anecdotes and sidebars and things he'd never said about them before – and still no one wanted him to stop! I ended up with over an hour of Bob on tape. Eventually the end had to come.

Thank God we'd had supper after Kate. And now people lined up to buy Bob's books and get them signed. An extraordinary scene. Helen and I had cleared up and Bob was still there – looking like he could have gone on another ten rounds with whatever – but he couldn't get hold of Juno (his wife). Kevin Clarke had sung to end the night's performing at ten to eleven. It was now after 11.30. Juno had left many messages and obviously needed to know if Bob was all right. Had she switched her phone off? It's hard for an outsider to appreciate simple arrangements between two people. Bob was so glad he'd brought the car closer at half-time now. He tried Juno's number again.

In March there were two visitors from Melbourne as guests – Steve Smart, arguably Australia's best performance poet, and Jennifer Compton, who was to win the prestigious Newcastle Prize for poetry later in the year. These two people have vastly different styles but I'd had visions of them somehow doing pieces together.

In her interview, Jenny talked about the theatre where she had her start and how she finds poetry a good outlet for dovetailing her several selves. Poetry and theatre were somehow joined in the subconscious but she preferred to leave any analysis about her output to the reader/listener.

It was hard to countenance Steve to a structured interview. He preferred to express through his medium, which comfortably took him over and resolved any angst about responsibility. He denied writing his bio on a recent website and I suspected Randall Stephens, who visited us with Steve in 2010. Steve was amused I still had his chapbook from that time (*Jars of Memory*). Maybe he'd have to 'find that person in that book again', he decided.

Several people expressed a willingness to contribute in turning Don Bank into a 1900s café in Montmartre in a special evening later in the year. One of those was Bee Perusco, who I'd seen before at Sappho Café and Word in Hand, Glebe – then she often appeared with a woman called 'Flower'.

This night she was performing with guitarist Allan Gallaway. Bill Tibben presented a mash-up poem using lines from his own and the poems of Maureen Ten and Danny Gardner from Maureen's anthology *Mood Lightning*. The trio, who perform as Running Order, were trialling the mash-up for insertion in a future program.

Two Bawdy Gentlemen – Ian Bryce and singer/poet Lee Cass – headlined the April Live Poets, swapping the mike from poem to poem, poem to song and back and so on, keeping it light and funny, then lewd! Limericks formed the preferred métier. This ditty from Ian was an oldie and a goodie about stray cats: 'Cats on rooftops / Cats on the Tiles / Cats with Syphilis / Cats with Piles / Cats with A-holes wreathed in Smiles – Because they're all thinking about the Fornication!' and so on.

After supper the other special guest – Evil Pesto – took over with the Blind Limerick Comp. Contestants called out a page number and had to read the piece on that page from a large book of the stuff. Several people declined because they didn't want to read rude poetry! People generally enjoyed the spirit.

In May the local Queen of Bossa, Anna Salleh, did a program of Brazilian-themed songs from her new CD. This was a miniature concert in effect, with bubbles and arrows of phrases and tones cocooned and energised in a rhythm that just would not stop. Samba and soul held dreams in a lilting waltz at other times.

After supper, Julia and Derek Parker, in an inimitable almost vaudeville style, took us on a dizzying journey in verse with poems down the ages demonstrating and reflecting on various signs in the astrological zodiac. It was a veritable movie for the ears – discoursing with dismay, disdain, desire and triumph through a succession of characters.

It was one of our more interesting programs of the year. It was a travesty I believe that only seven people attended this evening. In this week before the Sydney Writers Festival climaxed, people obviously wanted more straight poetry – was that the message?

The low numbers for June were more troubling. The night was billed as Something Intimate and featured Catherina Behan and Cecilia White. The performance of the former was personal plus, Behan's vulnerability accented by a cold. She is one of the better purveyors of intimacy around, and on the page the work is equally effective. Cecilia's was a cooler approach, more psychological, setting up an installation and inviting others to respond to it is more her style. It is an evolutionary practice Cecilia will continue in Paris next year. Having to engender a facsimile of that in words – even in interview – only doubled the difficulty for Cecilia. But engagement is what both these ladies are about, the audience undoubtedly richer for the experience.

But again there were precious few to witness it. There was a contention that people had stayed home distracted by the Labor Party power struggle ahead of the general election, even though that soap opera had some time to run at this stage.

In July there was something of a discussion through the work of Keith Hansen and Ariel Riveros Pavez respectively of Urban Myth: Virtual and Actual – the role of artistic competition and cooperation. Now, compare the online age of the social media blogger with the early 1970s when the process meant people inviting you to their studio to view work or meeting you in a café to discuss your poetry or, as musos did, joining a jam in somebody else's garage.

A contemporary of Brett Whiteley, Lloyd Rees and Martin Sharp in younger days, Keith was old school compared to Ariel, who ran several venues for music and poetry, and emceed forums through Elastic Sidewalk and other websites in a range of disciplines. Go online and find out more, was Ariel's motto. But were there any fewer secrets now? Did all the alternative media and chat rooms just act as agents for Self Promo Central rather than provide info people could share and benefit from? Did it really make it any easier for artists to contact each other?

This convenor weighed in with quotes from Iggy Pop and Alice Cooper, reminiscing how they hung out 'at Max's Kansas City' every night to meet musos in 1970s Manhattan. Keith also did songs and poems (and the artwork that dressed his CDs and the LP leaflet). Ariel demonstrated a facility for the Elizabethan madrigal and found poetry.

This night saw the return of Victor Ramos and memories of his Latin American Noche a decade or so before at Don Bank. Carole Kayat read a poem for the husband of an honour killing – a very challenging subject. John August took us out with an arresting Barcroft Boake (circa 1870s) poem: 'Where the Dead Men Lie'.

The big gate returned in August when we had a monster program – three guests: Kate Maclurcan with her new CD; Ouyang Yu, Chinese-Australian poet from Melbourne with his *Kingbury Tales*; and Pip Smith, who would read her work and adjudicate our inaugural Short Fiction Cup. I'd been angling for some time for Ouyang Yu to come visit again and his late notice in June was too good to pass up. He'd also provided publicity in the local paper when I mentioned in my press release his 'combative sometime controversial' style. The story made page 9! Kate had recently been wowing audiences from Mosman to Balmain with 'A New Day' and followed suit at Don Bank.

Ouyang rather dead-batted some leading questions in interview like: 'Why do you trade on being the Ungrateful Immigrant?' And 'Do you think [radical artist] Wu Wei is good for Chinese culture?' Plus 'Why can't China accept people's private worship?' (Ouyang had lost a brother who was imprisoned for practising Falun Gong.) His poems, however, were as uncompromising as ever. He finished with 'Someone', which detailed office workers' activity in the last few moments before the 9/11 planes made impact with the World Trade Centre towers.

Pip Smith has curated Penguin Plays Rough – evenings of storytelling – from intimate gatherings in Newtown to a social media phenomenon. She also talked about the Lifted Brow website to which she'd had to supply a poem a day without fail over summer, and read examples.

It was then time for our comp. The contenders were George Clark's 'Average Sex Life'and Marie McMillan (with heavy, breathy brogue) in her 'Tweeting at the Ashes'. (Shane was bound to star.) Bill Tibben with 'On the Edge', Susan Sleepwriter's 'Our Distracted Hands' and David May with 'Cliff Face' completed the line-up. Once all the contenders did their stuff, audience members had to vote by raising hands and George Clark and Susan Sleepwriter dead-heated. Clark won on a countback and he was duly presented with the short cup (painted up by Shuang the night before at home) to cheers around the room.

In September, Paris came to North Sydney. That is, we converted Don Bank's sitting room into the Lapin Agil – a

Montmartre café/cabaret circa 1906 – something of a precursor in its heyday to venues like Live Poets. There were storyboards of Lapin's history and influence. It was a hang-out for artists and writers, the artists including Picasso (with mistress Fernande Olivier), who lived in the nearby Bateau Lavoir of studio hovels, Toulouse Lautrec and Amedee Modigliani. The writers included Guillaume Apollinaire, Jean Cocteau, Max Jacob and (later) Dadaist Andre Breton. The famous cabaret singer Aristide Bruant actually owned the Lapin. The proprietor Frede, with the aid of his pet donkey Lolo (only overheard at Don Bank), perpetrated something of a hoax in the art world.

The impromptu Live @ Don Bank Players presented a performance featuring the above characters and their activities in Lapin's history. They were supported by Elyse (on French accordion) and song and dance musicians Bee (in a can-can dress) and guitarist Allan (period lounge suit). It was stimulating to see all the regulars and many others at Don Bank for the first time get into the swing in berets and sailor suits, fine gowns and hats in the French style.

Alistair Spate came as the poet Blaise Cendrars, replete with ceremonial cigarette attached to his face mask. There was sprightly senior Verdun Morcorm, who had some unusual talents as we would see later; Anthony Priwer; who came to play a French song on his ukulele; Des with his bird poem (Cocks and Blue Tits); Marie's Edith Piaf; Kate Mac there as a ravishing chanteuse – all the fun of the fair.

But now the players had to perform. Not being able to add theatrical lighting effects was a drawback. We got started with Dullin (George Clarke) singing brokenly, drunkenly declaiming old classics of the French symbolists as he commonly did at the Lapin. He was quieted by Frede (the convenor), who beat out some chords and sang 'La Vache Rit' until interrupted by artists Lautrec (Bob), Picasso (Gilmar) and Apollinaire (Bill T). Then Elyse with her accordion, making winsome eyes at Pablo.

Max Jacob's extraordinary, mincing portrayal saw Bob Howe donning a wig and putting rouge on his lips to cope! There was the court appearance of Picasso and Apollinaire (who had apparently colluded on the theft of three statuettes from the Louvre). Then Bruant (Bill T again) typically berating his patrons – and Lou Steer portraying Fernande Olivier's love for Pablo before Bee and Allan saw us to supper with can-can and café guitar.

The stage was darkened for part two as four friends analysed Pablo's controversial *Les Demoiselles d'Avignon* painting in secret. Jean Cocteau was all fresh in Bob Howe's hands and Apollinaire recited the 'Bridge at Mirabeau' before Andre Breton (Ray Wittenberg in a chauffeur's suit over which was hung a sandwich board splattered with eruptive manifestoes) invaded from Dada Land and ended up strutting and spouting around the room.

Finally, Frede is left to tell the audience about the Lapin's great scandal – Lolo the donkey's painting with her tail – that was trumpeted to a gullible avant garde as 'such a bold new style'! Frede then brings us quickly up to the present – for the Lapin is still there in a piano bar sort of glory in 2013. The cast at Don Bank, meantime, is called to take applause! It was either Don Bank's crowning achievement or a brave try! It was our third sell-out of the year.

Nancy Louka was the guest in October, along with much-published author Libby Hathorn and readers from the anthology: *Women's Work: a Collection of Contemporary Women's Poetry* which Libby collated with Rachael Bailey.

The open section called for pieces about Egypt, before Nancy's evocative defence of her homeland in her spoken word performance. In interview, Nancy said that basically we are from where we are from. And trouble for her relatives is trouble to her. This is the truth of a woman of her country. Nancy had a great sidekick in Gabriel Yakob, who backed her on guitar on a couple of numbers and executed a vivid paean to tranquillity at the end of her set.

The treat in the second half was Lyn and Rachel reading poems from the *Women's Work* anthology. There had been a call for contributors to come and read their poems too but only Ava Banerjee and Susan Adams complied. Lyn and Nancy had a fruitful link-up following this evening. Nashaa did a moving piece which epitomised for many how she started performing – the storyteller in a market place which could have been in Egypt. It was also Nashaa's way of saying goodbye – she was going back to Iraq for an indefinite time.

November was another vintage night – crowd near to capacity and a packed program. In the first part, A Walk Across Spain with Garcia Lorca, we had open section people doing their pieces about Spain interspersed with Lorca's poems about the same region. The above was backed by Gilmar Munoz's Spanish guitar and Mario Cabrera reading in Spanish and freestyling, at first from the sidelines and then inserting himself into the sequences. Several times I had to accommodate his admittedly sonorous Spanish – background to what our journey was about, surely. But Mario would not stick to a structure and with the night's crowded plate we couldn't afford to get sidetracked.

There were some moving pieces from Garry McDougall, who on the phone enthused about his daughter possibly coming to sing Spanish opera in the courtyard. Roberta Lowing's poem focused on the tragedy of Lorca's end and Phil Radmall applied Spanish philosophy to problems in a provincial English village.

The highlight for me had been inviting Verdun Morcom up to read a Lorca poem called 'Dream' with me. This classic two-hander materialises as one part of the brain talking to the other in the hypnagogic blurring a dream performs. I was the speculative partner and Verdun the rational and he was deadpan perfect as though we'd been doing it for years. He wasn't reading from a poem, he was just being.

Mario assumed centre stage again as I reflected on a ramble through a still Republican South in 1937. Gilmar closed the sequence with dramatic tones. Mario sat down but he wasn't finished. He began heckling guest Scott Sandwich after Scott and I had concluded a vivid interview. But Scott so subtly knew how to disarm Mario before the audience. The Patron Saint of Curtains (long story!) took off from there displaying the full proficiency of his art (I got phone calls of praise at home afterwards).

As we broke for supper, the night's other guest, Tineke Van der Eecken from WA, looked up at me and said, 'I don't want that man [meaning Mario] sitting there when I read.' In the event, Mario departed during supper with some help from Gilmar and Bill T. Tineke was sublime performing in several languages – musicality being the most enduring. Her repartee with the crowd was infectious.

The rest of the open section tumbled out long over time but no one was concerned. Bob Howe won the Orange Wig Award for his outstanding portrayals during Lapin and filling in at APWG. Lou Steer won the open section Poem of the Year for 'Stealing Paradise', about Robert Adamson's relationship with birds. It was inspired by that night in February. There was something of a ukelele muster over supper with Amory, Anthony and Jim Quealey in an impromptu jam.

Carapace

from bed
I see my clothes
on the chair
shirt draped over the back
collar crumpled
sleeves hanging
chino legs angled oddly
belt and buckle
suspended in space
all strangely vacant
today's empty identity

like cast-offs found
on the beach
abandoned carapaces
of scuttling sea creatures

I think of silent offices downtown
where chairs sit empty tonight
swung around at
odd angles
here and there
screen savers
blinking…blinking

back here
the cold side of my bed
is losing
day by day
the imprint of your body

when we step out of the
intricate artifices
of our lives
who are we?

Dexter Dunphy

Almanac

Panadol Tuesday.
The planets want me to make new commitments
but I've put my trust in ibuprofen.
You've accepted a divorce settlement: ergo, you're divorced.
Humidity – wind – pressure – boom!
Next time your father speaks to you you
better be more responsive you better lean forward.
It's the tudor classroom making a comeback,
treason and martyrology, consanguinity and incest.
How can I teach numerology to a bunch of
chuckleheads who can't spell alms.
It's like watching Ozu after work,
seasons come and go with their log of claims,
their pre-prepared obituaries,
the same silk blouse drying on the line.
Bring out the tea cups! Put away the abacus!
It's the perfect marriage of stamina and caprice,
dna and rooting powder following an inaudible trail
while all around us the bare branches are preparing to speak.
In Ueno Park office parties spread out under the trees
awaiting the first cherry blossoms.
A child conceived tonight will be blessed with patience
for checking facts, she will steal
hearts and keep them for a while,
she will grow old and bide her time.

Kate Lilley

Carnaby's Cockatoo

A wandering koel whistles
from a thicket of banksias, her eyes
circled with fire, her beak hooked

to dispense killing pecks.
The male answers, his call echoes
distance – scorned by other birds,

attacked by noisy miners.
Yeats' linnets remain as words,
as wings, were never here. Tonight

a flying fox eats warm apple pie
then flaps across dark suburbs
above a thousand swimming pools

with glowing chemicals.
The local apprentices
leave their hot cars up on blocks

and fork out for weekly bus tickets
to a factory's pervasive clock.
Pentecostalists pray to avian spirits

as they imagine cuckoos
flying from tree to thicker tree
into a world of lost chicks.

A pair of Carnaby's come and go
from a stand of melaleucas in a zoo –
they don't suffer noisy miners

and ignore the mystique of koels,
though still mocking them, drawing
from a screech the two infamous notes.

Robert Adamson

On the Waterfront In Genoa, Just Before Dawn, At Chucking Out Time

I asked the kids from Piazza delle Erbe who had led me here what the club was called because it had no sign. *Si chiama* Pussycats – they said.

It was two rooms in a warehouse up a flight of stairs. The music was loud. They had run out of white wine.

The kids took off and I sat myself down on a step made of stone. I didn't know where I was and had to figure out how to get home.

A young man, made of ebony, from Senegal or Somalia or the Côte d'Ivoire, sat down beside me gracefully.

Here you might think – Well well. But it wasn't like that. He sat next to me as if I was his mother, or his grandmother. I'm old. He was young.

I told him where I was from. He bent his head. Australia. Oh fortunate one. When I asked him about his country he leapt to his feet and sang.

Oh Mama…Mama Africa. Oh Mama…Mama Africa. He danced and sang. Then the tears came. A boy the age of my son.

I had a chocolate in my purse and I gave it to him. I don't think I know what hungry is. A stuttering and blind urgent cramming thing.

And yes, but don't tell anyone, I gave him the twenty euros that I had to hand. Stammering, ill at ease, he asked me what I had in mind.

It disgraced us both that he had to ask what the traffic between us was. But we strolled on. I bought him a stand up coffee at an early bar.

I had to order it because the girl wouldn't serve him. Her look of disdain. And then I said – *Goodbye, my friend.* And I went home.

Jennifer Compton

Seraphim's Dance

A grain of earth did pain the thrill
Mystery cries thus earth stood still
Tender flames lit Seraph's limbs
Our blessed Blue broke out in hymns
Soulful echoes in disguise
Drifting through them woeful eyes
A dark-end world; an unborn earth
Laud the Blue with joy and mirth
The dyeing hearts; Blue red hues
A silenced earth cried golden fumes
Awaiting stars; awakening birth
Seraphim's dance rejoicing earth:

> 'Rich the soul that wears the crown
> Amid the joyous woes that drown
> Trembling tears shall burn and burn
> To quench the soul with no return
> Amid the sorrowful joys and sighs
> From the dark-end ashes we shall rise
> To merging hearts that once did stray
> For 'Love', the hearts shall once obey'

Rainbow blisters
Teardrops did shake
Silent whispers
The earth did wake
Watchful conscience did grieve away
The soulful darkness of that day
Thus the fiery dance the Blue was given
O, mighty God! A newborn heaven.

Carole Abourjeili

This poem was translated into an art piece and sold to help victims of the Blue Mountains fires – embers of empathy via Red Cross.

Waiting

The first time we lay down together, your hands were nervous.
I felt your fingertips like butterflies on my hip and
I adored them – the weight of them –
the to and fro and tingle of them.
The exploration of them as we spooned, like it was nothing more than that,
like we could just be friends, lazing about on a warm day;
without thoughts of each other's skin, without our quickening
breath and wriggling bodies betraying our small talk.
Even now, your denial dipped words drip slow like honey and
I bite my tongue on the thoughts, on the memory.
If you want me, then admit it!
Wear each pulse and pull towards me like your favourite coat.
Wrap it soft and close around you.
Fish me out from your pockets.
I'm in there, gathering dust and rolling around in lint.
You can feel me – I see it in the furtive dip
of fingers just as quickly removed –
a child caught elbow deep in the cookie jar.
You lick me from your fingers and promise
you won't go back for more.
You leave us both wanting.
For what?
That mundane picket fence you sit on,
afraid to choose a side, afraid to fall
into these arms that wait for you, that want to teach you.
Instead we talk, and text, and describe late night scenes
that can never happen in the light.
That you would never admit to.

All the while it gets harder to
not touch, not tell, not trace that curve of neck to shoulder.
All the while you swallow your urges,
you shrug off your desires, you push me away and
pull me back and my should-know-betters get forgotten
All the while I wonder why
you throw away so much for something so ordinary.
All the while I wonder why
you return to him
with a clean conscience and wet underwear.

Catherina Behan

Eveleigh Street

The rusty triangle hung above
the withered gate
entices you to climb the stairs
of creaking jarrah wood.
Tread carefully
for under your weight
a soul that searches for a waiting train
rattles past and shakes the
molten windowpanes of
poverty palaces on Eveleigh Street.

Old man Tony, sitting perched
upon the orange crate,
tongues at the silver-chromed harmonica.
His jewelled eyes see no more past the
shoaled river's gate where once he
herded cattle to a shark-lipped
riverbank down south.
Scarce few foliaged trees
line the Redfern street
and yet a crack or two
can touch the cobalt blue
of cotton spun skies.

The rusty harp feeds the seeds of life,
the tongue that breathes and tastes the
sweet and sour.
Mrs Martin's clan has gathered in
the stained tile kitchen,
combustion burning in the cast-iron oven
and Bakelite decaying as the
urban rail, its time frame waltzing,
rattles teacups at the hour when
madams call the knights of vast
impossibilities and factories to share her
realm of calm delights.

I am offered from the open
Arnotts biscuit tin
sweet wafers from Pandora's box,
frankincense that bites the nose
and reeks of gin.
I kiss ladies' silk that touches
on my forehead
and opal earrings that weigh against
gold fillings of my niece's
cut enchanted smile.

Eveleigh Street, your matador
upon the Spanish orange crate, has found
a bed to calm eternity – and I,
the picador caught in life's traffic,
dodges FX Holdens and technology
that howls from the ghost of dull
electric shocks.

What can be done without love is only love's
ear, a tempered steel that listens to the
door of life; paper-thin walls of the
three-storey terrace house where the
clan has finished up the meal of
sacrificial lamb and famine fruits
of Irish lands.
So put away the plates of English bone,
dry them well before they go
into the cedar cupboard of the
parlour grand.
In April, May, June, aunties
saints and helpers who,
brush the cobwebs far aside,
return to dwelt-in suburban caves.
They offer now the ashes to
Eveleigh Street
where upon the guttered curb
the chromed harmonica lays.

Keith Hansen

An *anniversaire* of insomnia

Renter by night
come to live with
and disclose the lessons
of habitation by shadow
and of clear white moon.

No pedagogue for 5 a.m.
or the student romance
of overdue caffeine
and work

no duty to work itself
for automata of graveyard
shifts and penalty rates

no call to emergency services
or electrical substations under starlight

the unconscious just a flick
of a pilot light to an ordinary
beacon

yes and much is talked of in
dream, yet unlustrous are
scribed shells and the only sound
of sea is the neighbour's cough.

Angelus is the hour of three
and that's no cheat
in fact, it's a rotary
similar to the rest of the system

and responsibilities begin at 9
and break through the day
the lucidity of afternoon meals.

Only solitude can give
and only closeness can surrender
a correct word at the right time

but insomnia was never coming for you,
never would think to target you for its affairs anyway
to think so is grandeur
to sit through a night is not even a nothing.

Ariel Riveros Pavez

On a far journey

Before I set out on a far journey again
I put together
Bundles of those
Magazines that carry my poems
Those
Poetry collections that I have read
But don't want to read again, wishing neither to translate them
Nor to put down my thoughts about them
And those
New books that I can't sell
And don't want
To give away for free
In a big box
Some of them
I can't decide
If I want to take back
Such as the two new collections of poetry in English translation
I got published last year
Or the other two
On arts, literature and translation
Being torn between two countries
Is harder than between two women
As all one's time
Has turned into journeys
And all one's journeys
Into money
With one tossed in between
In the shape of a cloud

That has drifted to the edge of the skies
Oh, my aching heart
And there's no one to talk about it with
Now it occurs to me that those
Magazines
Will remain as rubbish
In the heap of odds and ends
One won't be bothered with again
Once taken home
How can life be such a tug of war
But, then again, one doesn't want to die
In a country
This unlucky

Ouyang Yu

Woman

Blood of my blood
Flesh of my flesh
Breath upon breath

I have known you in every language
translated the same across continents and seas.
You are the same
WOMAN
WOW
you are to me
Zan
Zena
Marrama
Lewa
Yinekes
ah-reh-la
Onna
Femme.

Gratitude
to the woman who awakes with ferocity
from her post-surgery sedate state
asking her children
'have you eaten?'
like a lioness tending to her brood.
True to maternal instinct.

Gratitude
to the woman
barefoot in South Africa
scarfed in Sudan
skeleton-like in Nepal
breastfeeding a newborn
or no breasts at all
to each his own crown.
I crown YOU.
Batigini – Strong woman.
It's your stride.
The way you ride.
Quench fires at the meeting of your thighs.
Luscious lips pressed upon cherry picked lullabies.

We failed to break you.
Broke back.
Beat-up.
Bruises birthed beauty.
Stretched skin.

Tone muscle.
Made you something like organic.
El natural born warrior.
Crowned Champion for life.

noorani (light of my eyes)
you taught me to pray
salt water pleads
for the men, we sometimes…
ostracise and name unworthy of rehabilitation.
Because some have…hurt people.
Hurt people hurt people.
Prayers ascend.
Blood of my blood.
Flesh of my flesh.
Breath upon breath.
Our birth cry
was never going to be our last.
And we'll be singing
till the heavens open up with thunder like redemption
for mankind.

Blood of my blood
Flesh of my flesh
Breath upon breath

When it gets too bad
I'll return to
your bosom.
Omena, our mother
Hodnek ausim
you have watered the earth from the blisters that
camp on the soles of your feet
nourished from the sap of your pain.
We thirst no more.
Our gain
Omena, our mother

Om el nour
Mother of light.
You sacrificed your own son.
And we still bitch about it like vinegar wasn't enough
on open wounds.

I am grateful for the lessons
that carve me into a better kind of me,
a better woman, beautiful reflections.
You hold a mirror to my face
saying 'look'.
I'm propelled into reflections of sight through your
eyes.
'I see'
and *te quiero* – I love you for it.

Nancy Louka

Wordless

I'm sorry if you're expecting something here.
Words are easy but words have been done.
I'm wordless.
It's been said better, it's been said sweeter
It's been said with more sincerity.
But it's not the words themselves that are the problem.

There's an earnestness I can't pull off
and a straight face I can't keep.
So I could say you're opulent or graceful
or you're the only thing that points north when I'm drifting
    off course.
And I know they're nice words.
But it's like my head and heart know that too.
And so I say nothing.
As beautiful as someone is, my problem is that
whatever I say will come out wrong if I don't *think* it
and meticulously choose, plan each word
but then where's the romance?

And far be it from me to propose a ground-breaking political
    statement
'Fear me not' 'Down with oppression'.
Right now that's not my place cause
I'm not beat or downtrodden,
and while that's a good thing, in the end
I'm a white man with a beard and a smile.

But I can string them together to tell you a story.
I can stop you from remembering I'm boring.
So I'll tell you something:
I'll tell you I'm hungry
to try and tell you I'm angry or sorry or hurtful
or point out my love will not be one grand gesture…but so
   simple that it stuns.

But I worry it'll come out wrong.
I know it's not too long.
But the space between my brain to my mouth to your ears
is too much for me to worry about.

So I'll keep it literal but with twists and second thoughts.
There'll be no confusion, just the occasional pun.
Because I'm wordless.

Scott Sandwich

For Séraphine

Ugiye he?　　　Where are you going?
Amahoro　　　Peace be with you
Umuzungu　　　White person

Ugiye he, where are you going, you ask
Kw'isoko, I say, I am going to the market
You laugh when I can't get the tone right,
when I don't say *isoko* but *isooko,* which means 'source'
like the source of the Nile

N'amahoro? Is there peace?
people greet us as we walk past the new election billboards
Children giggle and call me *umuzungu*
You've told me it's a word for white person, it means someone you only ever see
　　　　going past
like explorers, slave merchants, colonials
and aid workers in cars
I guess the word has not lost its meaning.

We stop to look at the newest *wax hollandais*, the latest fashion prints from Congo
while local *pagnes* wrapped in green, red and yellow, parade by
We work our way past rickety stalls made of tied bamboo
They sell bright orange palm oil in bottles, rice in any quantity you can imagine
and beans, beans and more beans
Amahoro ni meza, yes, there is peace, all is good

This market is as busy as a red anthill
We buy fish *capitaine*, Nile perch
Your kings live in the green hills, you say
never see lake Tanganyika
for fear of death

You don't greet the Batwa vendor

Then a word spreads through the crowd,
événements   events
événements
événements

'Events'. How very Burundian,
this euphemism for ethnic killings.
Vendors pack, vehicles toot and beep.
The crowd thins.
We follow the crowds across the street, past
Belgian shops, remnants of the past
People empty the shelves in fear
compete, for sugar, flour, rice, tea
and beans, beans and more beans.
For days the city pretends to be asleep

N'amahoro? No, there is no peace
There is fear in your voice
Don't worry, I say
we are here to bring peace
See – elections are coming
Multiparty democracy
You'll win, everyone will win
Amahoro   Peace be with you
You shake your head
You don't know this country, you say
I can't wipe the fear from your almond spiced eyes

What happens next only the tall grass on the hills can tell.

Ugiye he? – 'where are you going?'
Umuzungu – the one who is always on the move
N'amahoro? – is there peace?
Amahoro, umuzungu, ugiye he?   Peace, white person,
where are you going?

Tineke Van der Eecken

Sister green tree frog

Tree frogs
live green in toilet bowl:
free to roam from the septic tank buried in the yard to kitchen
floor to hunting living room.

The cubicle is palest green.
The toilet bowl is white. Drained by gravity plastic lid is open
most the night, serviced by two buttons, inhabited by green
tree frogs
dark night sit they on the seat
comes urgent need evacuate sits you in between.

Bright green grinning embryos live this salad life.
Hiding under rim of bowl from buttocks blue and white.
Big fat green thing in the pool flush one and two away
to septic tank again.

Like Cane toads in the yard. One night
frog sit where I want second swim in pool
one evade my finger feel
jump from heavy buttock to hand to paper roll.
Tissue stuck to green skin nothing good reveal, leaps again
onto cistern tank hides behind lavender aerosol.

I finish thing give cistern flush assign green tree frog number
two underground to cesspool.

Come the morn, sister shrugs, they find their way again
says natural oils from my hand does damage green tree skin.
I shrug my shoulders.
Frogs know what
like embryos need no womb
sometimes
when toilet bowl will do.

Ray Wittenberg

LIVE POETS AT
DON BANK

4TH WEDNESDAY OF EVERY MONTH (FEBRUARY - NOVEMBER)

5 NAPIER STREET, NORTH SYDNEY

$7 Admission includes supper and liquid refreshment
7.30pm - 10.30pm

INQUIRIES: (02) 9896 6956 or 0422263373 (mobile)
dannylivepoets@yahoo.com

All welcome to recite, sing, tell a story, play an instrument or just listen if you'd like to!

WEDNESDAY JULY 24 th
URBAN MYTHS: VIRTUAL AND ACTUAL

KEITH HANSEN
Paintings and poems tell your story of a place.

'Hollow Moon and Terrace Houses'

ARIEL RIVEROS PAVEZ
Blogculture is the lingo of a city's Matrix.

Elizabetha, Hip Hop, Auto-Pirate, madrigals

OPEN SECTION

LIVE POETS SUPPORTS REFUGEES

2014

Our first night of the new season was properly kicked off by the return of Paul Buckberry and his guitar, Paul telling us about his and his missus's band 'Faraway Eyes' and the release of their new CD at Bar Me, Darlinghurst, in a couple of days. Amory Hill was back with a piece about a nursing home inmate and poems from Stephen Herrick's *Caboolture* – the work of a 'real Australian poet' said Amory. Verdun Morcombe treated us to a remarkable piece born out of the swing and syncopation of Cole Porter's music.

Wiradjuri woman Brenda Saunders, our first special guest (she is an artist and a poet), told some vivid anecdotes about her time in France last year. The poems told of her childhood in Bullin Bullin, a place which can't actually be found now. We also learned of the origin of Sydney Aboriginal place names and compared what they have become – she has an artwork in Customs House which has modern Sydney real estate overlaid with tribal territorial designations; 'beware of Big Shark dreaming at Tamarama' is a line from one of her poems.

Philip Radmall, in interview, relived his fame as a bright young child of Albion (UK) in the early 1990s who, these days, is seeking to win the Newcastle Prize. He's come close twice. Like myself, half a decade earlier in the UK, Phil was taken up in the late 80s by the mixed-media mad Michael Horovitz. Michael published Phil in the anthology *Children of Albion* and I recognised lots of names I knew between the book's covers. Horovitz had a study you could barely stand up in Notting Hill (London) yet from there he networked his New Departures publishing and Poetry Olympics at the Albert Hall and knew everybody who was then anybody in performance poetry.

A 1920s eccentric in a 1980s outrage for a cause – that was

Horovitz. From nuclear war to the threat of global warming – yes, that long ago! Phil's poetry in Sydney has just got better and better. The novel writing (see Painting St Feoc from a couple of years before) might have fallen by the wayside.

Spectacle-wise, March took the cake for the year. Fifty people – many of whom had never clapped eyes on Don Bank before – turned up to see feature poets Susan Adams and Kaveh the Unlikely Poet from Iran.

Kaveh, an engaging mixture of physical strength and vulnerability of manner, turned the sitting room into something of a nightclub in the second half, with guitarists and backing singers and evocative lighting. This night had its organisational difficulties. On the Sunday before the meeting, Kaveh rang me to say there were seventy followers on Twitter who indicated they would be there – would Don Bank be able to cope?

Susan found herself reading in the first half to a sitting room that was heaving. The lads who couldn't sit down went to the courtyard and began making their own fun. Kaveh wondered aloud to a friend, 'What do I say to a North Sydney crowd?' But the fact that most of the attendees were from his own claque softened the blow.

I was grateful for Jack Peck going out to quieten the noise from the courtyard, though, while Susan read. The interview was a bit halting but she blossomed when she read.

We finished the first part of the evening with some numbers from Bee and Allan.

Over supper, the light crew, the tech support and the sound board were set up around the instruments and K asked about power outlets. The regulars crowded in at the back and after a quick stand-up interview, K eased into his sequence. It took us through the gamut of his work, quickly getting political (several people left at that point). Liberal politics, particularly their treatment of asylum seekers and the unemployed, was the principal target. K had recently attended rallies and demos about these and been feted for his impact. Other pieces turned to poems about his mother and love at university. A backing vocal to some beautiful guitar lent sculpture to K's more soulful moments, and the closing numbers could almost have been rock ballads. I eschewed the raffle and the other trappings to accommodate Kaveh's lengthy set, disenchanting some regulars no doubt, though Marie was not alone in voicing, 'That's real poetry!' Many people who came to see K came up to thank me for featuring him at Don Bank. Many others walked out beaming.

The blowback arrived via email the next day but it was not about Kaveh. It was a regular complaining about someone from the open section doing unsuitable (to them) material. I replied I would speak to the person concerned but we didn't censor – it was in our motto. That night I walked away to the car wondering how Don Bank could ever be quiet again. I liked that thought.

Birthday time again was 24 April! After the night of the Lapin Agil last September, I was quick to book Bee and Allan (Wilde & Free) for this party gig. They delightfully revisited Paris to invoke the Little Sparrow (Piaf) in an intimate torchsong around the patrons, then presented several gaucho songs in a cantina-by-candlelight style. They also pumped out the action from up front with two assistants, Clark Gormley on rhythm bass and Graham on guitar. The fuller sound suited them. On the other side of supper, they came back with an edgier effect – a war sound over 9/11 reverberations – then songs that told of a sea creature in distress and a ditty about working in a bank. They finished with a heartbreaker ballad of a doomed relationship, the refrain of 'you know I don't like ice cream' forming a soft mallet to the head.

We staged the second coming of the Monologue Challenge, where contestants drew speeches out of a hat with some intriguing results. For instance, Bob Howe was the Honest Whore (by Sheridan). Lou Steer was Alan Ayckbourn's double-glazing suitor in 'Man of the Moment'. Ava Banergee drew Richard, Duke of Gloucester, while Marie McMillan played the Roaring Girl. Garry McDougall was an Iraqi exile.

In what turned out to be an inspiring choice, Clark Gormley – before helping Bee and Allan do their thing – became 'Colon' Powell in David Hare's 'Stuff Happens', to such an extent that he took the top gong! You couldn't keep Clark out of the game – he took us out for the night as the singing pirate with coffee foam in his beard, and other grounds of concern.

Meantime, it was Shakespeare's 450th birthday. Elizabethan street music greeted patrons coming in and this convenor offered scattered echoes of Elizabethan street life: from the cutpurse, the reveller, the dowager – how to kill fleas and walk on water, test a witch – and a song about the Plague in Cheapside.

May was a night of travel poetry, with special guest Jacqueline Buswell reading from her book *Song of a Journeywoman*. The night was called Caravanserai (an inn in a desert). The PR leaflet featured one of this convenor's favourite paintings: Paul Klee's view of Kairouan, Tunisia, which has one the world's most famous caravanserais. However, Jacqueline's book was principally about travels in South America.

Meantime, I'd come across a beautiful book of old travel posters and scenes from Mexico and made up a posterboard for J to that effect! She was rather feisty in interview – denying travel poems were all happy. 'There are ups and downs like normal life – you do have incredible highs.' Do travel poems, like stories, have to have a thread, a back story? 'I don't believe these are travel stories. My journey is a journey through life. We travel also when we hear the evening news. I've written about Baghdad often but I've never been there.' Jacqui explained she got out of the UK and went to Mexico for a change of weather – 'and stayed there (and other parts of South America) twenty years.'

Journey started with poems about country, proceeded to song then streets and a sense of injustice before reverting to song on the road home. The audience was a willing limpet on her baggage!

We'd already been treated in the open section to Des Spensa's experience at the barricades, Eilleen's passage to 'Tir Na Nog', and visited Amory Hill's 'ghosts in heaven'. Post Jacqueline, Helen Wren read T.S. Eliot's 'Journey of the Magi', newcomer Jenny boarded an airport bus to learn about mathematics, Fadeel played a tribute to dear departed friend Nashaa on flute. And we got NASA's views on David Bowie's *Space Oddity* via the *New Yorker*.

June saw Don Bank feature Auburn Poets and Writers' *Welcome to DisPlace*, fresh from the SWF, in two halves bracketing supper – although a couple of people in APWG's previous gig were absent and Don Bank regular Bob Howe took the place of Willem Tibben, who was away in the Kimberleys.

After the performance, Bhuppen Thakker recited a very moving tribute and Nancy Cheng said, 'I've really enjoyed this evening.' She won the *Women's Work Anthology* in the raffle and promptly passed it to APWG's Isil Cosar in thanks. The night also included some Biennale Browsing reports and a tribute to Seamus Heaney. Phil Radmall offered a poem on Heaney's death. Des's example pitted schoolwork against the simple toiling man in Heaney's 'Digging'. Bob did a Heaney poem about ironing. Brigitte, Phil's partner, one about Valentine's Day. George's partner read a poem about 'Arabian Horses'. Roberta Lowing, on a rare visit, did a piece from her new book on a victim's persistence.

July Live Poets saw the Night of the Mask with Kyla Ward magnetising attention from her first walk through the darkened room from the front door, holding only an electronic candle. In the following thirty-minute display, both chilling and dexterous, Kyla held the audience spellbound to an extent I have rarely witnessed. In her depiction of a bird dissecting a cadaver, for instance, mouths hung agog. Her duet with Marie McMillan, as kittens trying to deceive their master, by contrast, was a source of hilarity.

The launch of *Stars like the Sand*, a volume of speculative poetry, was next. It was disappointing that more people weren't on hand to read their contributions and the co-editor had to call in ill. Interactive Publishing's David Reiter took us on an insightful voyage through his groundbreaking memoir *My Planets*, which included the anecdote of his mother being schmoozed by Frank Sinatra's minder. Over supper there was the Masked Bards Ball in the courtyard to the strains of Johann Strauss and Ricky Martin.

August was billed as a Home Fires night, with the second running of the Short Fiction Cup plus other exercises in Reading the Blues and What Makes Your Poem Gel? It was one of the venue's lowest attendances of the year and it seems the Cup will have to be supported by a special guest in future. That said, the comp featured some good talents plying their wares.

Defending champion George Clarke was in hospital with back problems but sent a story, 'Welcome to My Nightmare', for someone else to read – Des Spensa's partner, Jo. Des himself performed 'Letter to My Grandchild', which tried to explain why his generation was unable to combat climate change successfully. Bill Tibben offered an anecdote about a family car trip, while the redoubtable Verdun Morcombe told of his stint as a journo in the UK in the story 'Flinders to Fleet Street'.

Kerry Jamieson it was, however, who took home the special

cup with her story 'Storm'. But again – like the first time – there was a re-vote after a tie between Kerry and Verdun.

In 'Reading the Blues', poets had to resist the urge to sing some very danceable lyrics as Bill T grappled with 'Go Down Moses' and Verdun Morcombe inhabited 'Chicago Mill Blues'. In 'What Makes your Poem Gel' and so on, Bill T gave us an instructive analysis of his 'In a Supermarket in Epping', which took as its model Ginsburg's 'In a Supermarket in California', with G following and trying to 'catch up' with Walt Whitman. Des then chatted about how he hit on the spoonerisms that gave his 'Cleopatra's Sphinx' some muscle. Lastly, Danny told of how he arranged the tableau of a gull crying in the moonlight and an old man who couldn't sleep in his bedsit to 'fix' The (Neutral Bay) Wharf of 1916.

There was a good general discussion about composition with old friend, Arabic poet Shawki Moslemani, before the meeting started. 'When the poem is ready to write you, it can happen anywhere' said Shawki. 'Poetry is so often about the past and holding things in your head – until you think this may be the last poem you write.' Des said, 'You've got to get started and then it takes over.' Shawki, 'But when I give it to the publisher to translate, I wash my hands. It's up to him.'

On to September and there were three guests booked. Mark Tredinnick came to pay tribute to the fact that language is continually on the move – as 'we are all coming from somewhere else in a way'. He was also saluting England's tradition of lyric poetry – the reading was headed Homage to Our Native Tongue – especially in the work of Mark's mentor, Gerald Manley Hopkins. Mark was as usual generous with his rich observations and examples illustrating his concepts – though he was stumped when I quoted him: 'We are tragic mortals living in an immortal world' – could he expand on that a little?

Kristin Hannaford read from her book *Icon*, which was concerned with some famous Sydney collectors of 'preserved animal resources' in Victorian times. Randall Stephens, on the cusp of heading to WA and cycling across the Nullarbor to raise awareness of 'Haemophilia', began prosecuting his latest book *One for the Road* with his poem about finding 'the biggest sky to do it under' – if you want to be lonely.

A welcome visitor was Hamish Danks Brown, finally able to make it down from Maroochydore after enjoying our reviews on Facebook for some months. Marie McMillan made a Hopkins poem 'sing' and reminded us of the fine melodies in English poetry we've all suckled on at some time. Kerry Jamieson used Yeats to engender a little humour – a good way to go out. Bee and Allan had laid down some wicked guitar and vocals to get the evening started.

There was the sadness of the recent passing of Martin Harrison and I read a poem of his from the venue's last anthology. Later, Mark T reflected to me how he had taken so many times himself the same road where MH had suffered his fatal heart attack while driving home to the Central Coast. The eeriness he experienced during his next transit of that place – after hearing what had happened to Martin – was palpable.

In October it was time to go back to Manhattan, in 1980, to the Lips Inside Speakeasy on the Lower East Side. The room was bedecked with images from the convenor's 1980s New York scrapbook. He then performed excerpts from his memoir of the time, wandering nocturnal streets among a calvalcade of passing characters, before he collided with music from the NY Dolls and other Punks at that bar – their lyrics in 2014 read/sung by volunteers to backing by guest garage-guitarist, Dirk Kruithof.

An added drama in the lead-up to this event was Dirk's partner expecting but, sensibly, the coming baby knew to hold off! Who were these volunteers performing with Dirk? Bob Howe enacted 'Trash' by the NY Dolls. Lou Steer did 'Lust for Life' by Iggy Pop. Lou Reed's 'New York Conversation' was interpreted by Phil Radmall. Television's 'Marquee Moon' got the treatment from George Clarke. Talking Heads' 'Life in Wartime' was taken on by Fayroze Lutta.

Afterwards, local performance poetry icons Candy Royalle and Omar Musa strutted their stuff. Candy stood on a chair to deliver a rendition of Patti Smith's 'Rock n Roll Nigger' over the audience's rising cheers and foot stomps. Omar took a deep breath after that finale to propel us on an emotional rollercoaster – from outsiders' rapper anthems to mouth-watering invitations to soul food and a paean to Lady Day (Billie Holiday) which featured this line: 'we all die, we all yearn, we all shine, we all burn'.

This was all on before supper because Omar had a 6 a.m. start the next day. He was off to Japan with his mum. He enjoyed a few wines over conversation and supper nevertheless. Zoe Dobson scored Dirk's CD in the raffle and we rolled on in part two with a massive open mike. A highlight was Ember Flame's evocative narrative in verse in tune with the night's feature 'In New York you can be Anyone.' Fayroze Lutta's 'Bathurst Street' was a fine example of urban mythology in our own fair city.

November was set aside for people to react against the Liberal Murdoch government in Reflections of Abbottaphobia. This opportunity to vent in verse had been pushed for by several people since early in the year but on the night itself, Bob, Roberta, Des and Lou, where are you? How many Liberal voters *are* there among the Live Poets regulars? What about the recent loss of the poetry program *Poetica* on the ABC – hasn't *that* fired up the rebel loins? (Come in, Barvara!)

Special guest that night, Erwin Zehentner, reflected on

this ABC cuts thing later. 'Only 1 in 10 people listen to poetry compared to 3 out of 10 who won't be able to watch the Shute Shield (rugby) in the future.' Other people told me, 'Those people in government are not interesting enough to drive you to verse!'

Erwin had a sculpture of Tony A – a faceless man with a tin ear and one eye who 'dressed' to the surf lifesaver's bias and watched the whole proceedings in silence! Erwin's chief business was to lend insight to the life and poems of Austrian poet George Trakl (revered by Robert Adamson for one) who died about a hundred years ago of a drug overdose. Erwin and George shared a hometown (Salzburg) and an occupation in chemistry and E laced his presentation with sometimes meandering anecdotes.

There was also a tribute to Dylan Thomas, who was born during the Great War's first weeks. Ed Wilson responded with a poem about visiting Dylan's birthplace. Jack Peck read 'Do Not Go Gentle', which reflected on a bit of his own family's folklore. And in the open section, Yarrie Bangura finally made it to Don Bank to reflect on how Australia became 'my home from home'.

This convenor took us under the shadow of the MH17 plane disaster and the Russia–Ukraine, war using poems from U's writers, recently apprehended at a Sydney Mechanics Institute presentation headed by Tania Bonch. The surreal camera-eye view of one poet in particular created a graphic disembodying effect when performed.

But to get back to Abbottaphobia. Bee and Allan did a song about David Hicks and Guantanamo, oddly born as a protest at how the issue had dominated water-cooler conversations at the time! I then read a limerick about Julie Bishop's Ship of Truth Foundering on the Great Barrier Reef and a group of us read the new national anthem under Abbott – sample: 'for we are white and free…and we lock up refugees'.

Ember Flame's piece from October, 'In New York You can be Anyone', was announced as the open section poem of the year.

We did all the above before repairing to the courtyard for supper, the raffle, the Un-Darwin Awards and an after-party – chiefly centred on artists' clutter and how it reflects on their genius.

There was also a competition where people were invited to respond in word and song to a Martin Sharp painting depicting Marilyn Monroe and a Van Gogh vase from the Art Gallery of NSW's current exo Pop to Popism. Kerry Jamieson took the gong with a poem/song including elements of Don McLean's song 'Vincent'.

Sonnet

in memory of Ruby Hunter, singer-songwriter, 1955–2010

Ruby sings a black girl's music
shares a song of loss and longing.
Her tiny frame sways to the beat
sobs a low note deep inside.
A honey-roll voice shares the pain
of a river girl's yearning. Taken
as a child to the strangest places
far from life on the old Coorong.
She calls up music she once heard
women singing at the campfire.
Rituals of her birth one night
the billabong holding the moon.

Ruby sings her longest journey
calls the Ngarrindjeri home.

Brenda Saunders

Coleface

with respect to Cole Porter

It's the wrong time,
And the wrong key,
But the chords are anything but shonky.
They're such *hip* chords.
They should be played at Lords,
And they might work in C.

Songs by Porter
Give no quarter,
Situations rise which hadn't oughta.
And if *his* words
Antagonise the birds,
Reposition the tree.

B flat diminished,
One half step down,
Suggesting a mystery unsolved.
And when that bit's finished
I'm off into town,
The gin with the tonic resolved.

They may clap ya
And gift wrap ya,
But you know for sure you won't fool
APRA.
Diatonic responsibility
May yet settle on me.
So it's all right,
I'm up all night,
But it's all right
In C.

Verdon Morcombe

Dodgy Dick the Fracking Engineer

I stopped at a little town called Tara to have a quiet beer,
I saw a bunch of blokes with fat wallets and grins from ear to ear.
They were talking about a great treasure that they had just found,
On some local farmer's paddock deep underground.
As I watched and listened one guy was louder than the rest,
He talked of oil and gas and getting rich with great zest.
The publican saw me watching and came over for a chat,
I asked who the clown was wearing the black cowboy hat.
The publican looked quite sad as he poured me another beer,
And said that was Dodgy Dick the Fracking Engineer.
He came up here and offered the council great riches,
They signed an iron-clad contract with him the bloody sons of bitches.
It all started quite simply when they gave a farmer twenty grand,
To drill a few small holes upon his dad's best farming land.
They bought in bulldozers and big trucks with rigs to bore,
They built roads everywhere and drilled holes by the score.
They built those bloody wells to extract coal seam gas they said,
They used all the town's water and put one near my backyard shed.
I can't sleep at night with the noise and my chooks have given up laying,
My missus said it's made the kids sick and she's doing lots of praying.
My mate Bill said they dumped fracking fluid in his northern creek,
It poisoned all the bushes and killed some of his sheep.
The greenies and scientists say it'll ruin the Great Artesian Basin,
Poison all my drinking water and get Global Warming really racing.
The politicians have turned a blind eye to what's happening up here,
We'll make heaps of money they say, there's really nothing for you to fear.
So if you blokes down south don't want to suffer our sad fate,
Say NO to Dodgy Dick the Fracking Prick, and lock your Fracking Gate.

Des Pensable

43

declared missing not dead   yet they search for them
in clandestine graves

43 student teachers
who lost their future and whose future students lost them
who lost their mountain homes and the mountains
lost the echo of their voices
they lost their lives and a nation woke, cried *basta*

the people cry   *you took them alive*
we want them alive

they protest the disappearance of the 43
and of tens of thousand others
kidnapped, gone forever missing
neither dead nor alive   for friends and families

some protesters have no language for loss
they´re burning down the house

one hundred years ago Mexico had its revolution
that lasted years and claimed two / three million lives
decades of disquiet and uncertain peace ensued

but the war on drugs broke that peace
claimed 60,000 lives and more
who can say how many?

clandestine graves are scattered across the nation
several uncovered since the 43 disappeared
have proved to hold remains of many
other unfortunate citizens   gone missing

a routine student demo went so wrong
it woke a nation shouting
down with the narco state
and left all those parents grieving

Jacqueline Buswell

Herbal Tea

Goblins sleep in the roots of herbs,
where cats' eyes peep in the roots of herbs.
Intricacies of tiny limbs,
of crawling, gnarled and hidden things.
Secret juices, fragrant life,
a monkshood and an iron knife
cross uneasy over the fey
rustles from the dim-dawned day.
Leathern books and old proverbs,
shadows creep in the roots of herbs.

Goblins hide in the roots of herbs,
careless bride in the roots of herbs,
garland-winding lost her way
forever; taken, here she lay.
Imprisoned, mingled, roots her grief,
her veil became the scented leaf
and in the earth the unkissed wife
found no grave but stranger life.
She waits by overgrown herbs.
Secrets sighed in the roots of herbs.

Goblins lurk in the roots of herbs,
uncanny work in the roots of herbs.
Precious powers hold that stem,
strange aches of flesh are linked to them.
Feathered shard of root so round,
drawing deep to underground.
Kitchen windows, walls of brick,
in pavement cracks the hint will stick.
From castles to decayed suburbs;
oh, never shirk the roots of herbs.

Goblins watch in the roots of herbs,
for lore will cost in the roots of herbs.
Fear to enter such a maze
where distilled ichors cure or craze.
Seductive leaves their fragrance waft,
a half-seen hand, a hidden laugh,
and when such things are known to me,
what should I drink but herbal tea?
A toast! To all that peace disturbs,
and children lost in the roots of herbs.

Kyla Lee Ward

Haiku Walk

Ormiston Gorge, Northern Territory

Red-tailed dragonfly
sunlight chink in marble rock
find your way through it.

Tiny white daisies
adorn the red cathedral
waiting for the bride.

Red gum branch on sand
many stories in your bark
tell me your secrets.

Helen Wren

Wild Wind

Heavy is the weight of snow and wind,
heavier is the weight of invasion
on innocent territory.

The fence around the farm is breached,
The limits overrun.

Marauders constantly come into the farm,
they come to shed the blood of simple farmers

They come for land, for power.
They want to conquer all,
take all, own all.

They step on hopes and dreams
they step even on the sleeping
and the unborn.

Birds leave the farmland,
even birds with broken wings
struggle to escape.

This army of the night
encircles every blameless throat
and takes its deadly meal.

This army of the night
pillages society,
pillages its soul.

Life continues, life goes on.
Only bitter memory repeats,
repeats, repeats.

Assad Cina

Dancing Sinatra

I have to pinch myself. Here I am, about to knock on Frank Sinatra's door at 2 a.m. I don't know what to expect. No, I do know what to expect, but I'm still here!

He's promised me the last dance. In his room. The top floor in the Ritz Hotel. Will there be room for the band, too, or will we hum a slow dance cheek-to-cheek?

I put my ear to the door and hear…nothing. Is that a good sign?

When I knock, a tall man opens the door. He's a bit of a grease-ball, very handsome and muscle-bound, but he's not Frankie.

I look around him, into the dim.

'Come in, Miss,' he says politely. 'The boss is expecting you.'

'Where *is* the boss?' I ask, wondering if this is Frankie's room at all.

'On his way,' the man says, walking inside. 'My name's Reg. I'm to look after you until he gets here.'

'And how long is that likely to be…Reg?' I say, following him.

'As long as it takes,' he says. 'Hungry?'

There's the faint smell of Italian food lingering in the air.

'What's that smell?' I ask.

'Eggplant Parmigiana,' he says. 'Frankie made it, especially for you.'

'Oh, really,' I say. 'And when would he have done that – between acts?'

'This morning,' Reg says, trying to stifle the grin. 'Don't know how he knew you was coming but he did!'

'Lots of garlic?' I say, playing along.

Reg rubs an imaginary bit between his thumb and forefinger. 'Only the smallest bit, in the tomato sauce. Frankie's a genius with parmesan!'

'I'll bet you say that to all the girls!' I say.

'Only the ones he cooks for!' he winks. 'Want some?'

I nod and sink into a chair. It smells like perfume. Fresh perfume.

He was right about the parmigiana. Two glasses of champagne
later, still no Frankie, and Reg is getting *very* friendly.
'What if Frankie comes in?' I say, trying to hold him off.
'Something tells me,' Reg murmurs, 'that he's been held up. But I
can pass on the good word for you – in the morning.'
By then, I was so tired that, Frankie or Reg, it hardly made any
difference. And Reg didn't seem to mind the garlic on my breath.

David Reiter

Footlock

I want to dance the tango
But to do so I need a man,
A man to lead and guide me
To show me off, if he can.
But finding a leader's not easy
Though flexible I may be
For the tick list's quite demanding
In order to partner me.

My *tanguero* may be a tad taller,
Though not necessarily so.
His chest must act as a semaphore,
Signalling, ubiquitously, as we go.
His age is a matter of irrelevance,
Place on sexual spectrum – let's ignore,
English proficiency quite inconsequential,
Though arms, feet and torso must score.
Grasp of Argentine history not mandatory,
But innate musicality's the core.

'Twas a dance born in a bordello
Truly brings quite the tart out in me
As I'll slither down his front in a *colgada*
Or glide rather suggestively.
Now a shoulder lift's almost impossible,
If Herculean strength has not he.
Near-horizontal's not always advisable
So I'll stick close to verticality,
To a partner without halitosis
Who deodorises regularly,
And I promise to give him a shoeshine,
To caress slowly, with solemnity,
Bony ankles, his metatarsals
Will rub quite provocatively
Till he's desperate to be my *tanguero*,
A fit leader for li'l' old me.

And I swear that I never will tell him
Of my heinous hypocrisy,
For all I want is a partner,
That is, someone who's willing to be
The epitome of a gentleman…
Who'll embellish me, pe dal ly.

Marie McMillan

Storm

The bellbirds' voices rise pipe-piping up from the valley floor, over the creamy sandstone bluffs and cliffs, clear as lightning and hollow as an old tin can. Olive and beige wrens zip their way through the bristling bushes and come close-as-you-dare to the curious walkers. Sprinklings of gum nuts litter the soil, and the grass-trees' green quills spike into the air like a porcupine's. A hoard of blue Biro lids and bottle caps, pegs, straws and plastic scraps – a bowerbird's showy stage – leads the way to a lady's heart. A streak of orange, pale and deceptive in its suggestion of heat, underlines the evening sky.

Come evening the wind is gusting in the great gums and shaking the little houses. Loose leaves leap the gutters, and boughs wave an unwelcomed hello. Fledglings are thrown from their nests to lie with their final squawks on an unforgiving ground. The locals scurry home, heads hunched, the vengeful cold biting their hands and purpling their lips. No amount of coat can keep them warm.

They tune in to crackling televisions. 'A marked low pressure system lies over south-eastern New South Wales tonight. Winds of up to 120 kilometres per hour may be expected in the Blue Mountains…' Unwatched pots boil over and fireplaces crack and hiss. The children's stories are dark tonight and full of trolls and witches.

The old woman is lying propped up on paunchy pillows, coughing hard. The hospital windows are scungy with rain-spattered dust and spider webs. For company she has the wretched waiting and waiting for the final dreaded, expected day. Do you want to be here? she asks her daughter. Yes, the daughter lies. But she has been there every day for this past punishing month and her generosity has worn thin. She wanted a mother who was soft and feathery around the edges. Yet pictures appear unbidden of flying through the air to smack against a wall; tears every bedtime; and insults and attacks, despite the trusting and helpless love of a child. The bad memories are drowning the good as the old woman's lungs are drowning in a deadly pool of sticky secretions.

The wind whips around the telegraph poles. She is gasping now. At last her eyes close as the rattling breaths come more slowly. The son, conveniently arrived recently from a European holiday, comes in to pay his last respects. The storm sings its last harmonies through limp, rusty clotheslines.

Death slides in like a whisper. Release. A latex-gloved hand draws the sheet, and the old woman is on her way to the coldest room in the hospital. All is quiet except the swirling sound of the polisher on the carbolic-acidified linoleum floor. Outside, the bowerbird slowly pieces its nest back together and the piping of the bellbirds tentatively pierces the air.

Kerry Jamieson

Nursing Distraction

Can you hear this? I imagine it is the sound
electricity makes, a kind of crackling, the fizz
an anode might make if it were inserted into my heart.
No one is listening.

Do you see this? The walk of zombies.
The dead held at the impasse of traffic lights,
at bus stops and in school yards. Each quiet
domain mediated only by the daylight blue
repeating on the screen before us,
as though we are not standing here together
the eclipsed moon not above us, hidden by the clouds.

Kristin Hannaford

Are We There Yet?

Are we there yet?
My voice is so whiny
in the back seat of my head.

In the front seat
I drive past
shadow landscapes

and neon signs
promising
around the next corner
a realer, better life.

We can't be far off now
I say
though I'm scared
I missed the turn-off.

Siri had such
convoluted directions
for lasting love
and motherhood

now the road is lonely
there's static on every station
and my hands
are sweaty on the steering.

I just want to arrive
at that place I booked
strength
success synergy.

Or else drive into a ditch
and have someone
very heavy lie on top of me.

This car is a bomb
I bitch from the back.

I sigh.

And wonder if this journey
would be easier
in a family sedan
self-delighting convertible
or monster truck
on methamphetamine.

I floor it
into compressed darkness
now no vision
just a line of broken white
and the stars to guide me.

Night mobs
the cool dew windows
and charcoal angels sneak in
singing favours
of death change
forgiveness, patience

they kiss
our crumb-lined car seats
and I close my eyes
for tall towers of seconds
without veering off the road.

I slow down.
I think I've hit something
perhaps epic peace
but it falls away

so I pass a bag of chips
back to myself
and count down the kays.

Ember Flame

The Connoisseur

with apologies to Robert Balas

Good evening, sir, how are we tonight?
Welcome to the Gallery.
May I recommend, for your enjoyment
A light bubbly white, not quite French, but
I believe the wine maker once spelt France correctly,
We do have some relationship.

Perhaps, a little light Impressionistic offering?
Nothing too challenging, first up. Must warm up, so to speak.
Followed by a flinty Sauvignon Blanc, so at one,
With the Mondrian, or is it a Braque, I can never tell.

Then perhaps, we should try a light Shiraz,
Nothing too trying, mustn't overtax the brain
The abstract expressionists will do this anytime.
A bit of chromatic, gestural, I think my head hurts.

Now we come to the piece de resistance, the classics
Nothing like a well-rounded Cabernet Sauvignon, or Merlot
To go with some well-rounded ladies by Brueghel or Rubens
To top off the night

It has been a wonderful night, thank you
But there is one thing missing
I never saw the Quadratic Polymorphisms?
Believe me Sir, you will, particularly if you miss
The non-linear Dynominals, and finish up on your
Hyperbolicity, in the gutter.

Erwin Zehentner

Note: the strange words refer to Chaos and Pendulum theories as once related to Pollock's work.

Our Distracted Hands

She is part-lizard. Just the breath of a breeze sending her scurrying into corners and woollen coats. Her impenetrable hide, tougher than teeth, jibes running free from her glossy flanks. Yet look closely and you will see the sucking, in and out, of the heart beneath her skin.

We should never have gone out in the boat. I know that now. Out of scurry-distance from home. Exposed to the elemental wind, where even the salt-encrusted deck held the taunt of ice. I blame myself. I had no resistance to the lure of wind tugging at my feathered arms, the horizon spreading as I sailed the updrafts. Let's go! My insistence, beak-sharp, squealed like gulls for fish and chips.

We argued over the mangoes. Vehement and incessant, as the sea heaved beneath us. As if those mangoes had taken years to ripen, coddled and caressed by our attentions and intentions. As if carried tenderly in our quivering skin, through late night conversations, cushioned in assumption. Then later tossed, clumsily between us. Our distracted hands. Yours tightening the tourniquet to feed your hungry veins. While I grew fat with loss.

I don't know how we got the boat back to land. The threatening indigo horizon. The touchstone of the wharf vanishing in the swell. The hurling of jagged words, like hail. All sounds deadened by the roar of our faces in their hollow-eyed masks.

That boat now rests somewhere on a distant shore. If you look closely you will see a feather sticky with the pulp of mango and just the briny stain of a lizard's frozen tear.

Susan Sleepwriter

I am Jamal Al-Hallaq

My name is not an elegy.
Maybe next few months
My country will disappear
From the world map
Exactly like Yugoslavia
Few months and no more Iraq
In the news.
They will talk about
Cities and villages
Cults and tribes.
They will talk
About all the fragments.
But no one will remember
That country that once
Invented writing
In one of its ancient dreams.

Jamal al Hallaq

Home Away From Home

Ripped from my homeland like an unrooted tree
Transplanted to a new land
Here I took root
As the suffering of my homeland lingered
Severed limbs scattered
Like jagged, discarded branches.
I stand on blood-soaked earth
My feet caked in gore
Frantic with horror.

Running into the arms of Aunty Australia
Scattering seeds from Mama Africa
The earth is cool and green
The waterlily shoot from the mud.
Aunty received me with open heart.
Innocence revived.

A storm rumbles,
Shadows of a black cloud from years of war.
The drumming of heavy rains
That salty veil of tears
The many sins of war.
The wild waterlily blooms
Seeds from Africa come to life
On foreign soil
Silted with memories
Of braided hair.

My life becomes clearer, I grow stronger in mind
The petals outstretched, waving in the sun.
The vibrant colours that move in a
Kaleidoscope of dance.

Yarrie Bangura

Poetry and Presenting it in Public Part Five

Is poetry above politics?

Martin Langford: No. Fashions in opinion shape the reading space much more comprehensively than we like to admit – and not just overtly political opinion.

Willem Tibben: No. Politics is below poetry.

Richard James Allen: Poetry is better than politics. But everything is political at some level.

Candy Royalle: Again, I don't understand this question. Above politics? Art is political.

Susan Adams: Above? Yes!

David Falcon: The poetry that I am interested in is above politics in the same way that love, compassion and empathy are above politics. This is not to say it must never seek to teach or promote a cause but that it must have, at its heart, a shared human experience.

Paul Buckberry: Poetry is a human form, so is politics.

Phil Radmall: It sits amongst everything, and provides a response.

Les Wicks: Above politics? No.

Benito di Fonzo: Entirely up to the poet. However, I personally think that politics is just another word for human relations, interactions, so in that sense everything is politics. Whenever I communicate to another person, that is a political act. And poetry is a form of communication, so…

Scott Sandwich: Poetry can sit wherever it wants, wherever the poet wants it, wherever the audience wants it. Not all poems have to be timeless. If you want your poetry to be political or partisan, go for it.

Cathy Bray: Some poems are purely political but poems on the five senses or landscapes or daily tasks or universal emotions which appeal to all human beings are beyond politics.

Edwin Wilson: Who would imagine there was ever politics in poetry? Poetry, sadly, like most other human endeavours is not pure and unsullied, and above politics – as humans – as social primates – are very tribal, very 'them and us'. Poetry has always been subject to vogue and coterie and has always been notoriously faction-ridden – at the point of intersection of self-righteousness, entitlement, ambition and envy. As demonstrated by the Ern Malley hoax and the fights between the traditionalists and the modernists, and the anti-communist crusades. Religion has been very much in this mix as well. The poet Shelley was thrown out of university when they were controlled by the churches, for publishing a pamphlet on atheism. William Tyndale was exiled and pursued by Catholic authorities and strangled and burnt at the stake for having the audacity to translate the New Testament into the English language. There have always been the thought police and culture wars and taboo words, when the killer word today could well be 'jihadist'… The Scottish Martyr Joseph Gerald – buried in the Sydney Gardens – had been transported on a charge of sedition. One of his crimes had been to use that verboten word 'citizen'. The word 'comrade' killed careers in the 1950s in the USA. My own career as poet had been almost strangled before it had happened through shrill charges of 'chauvinism' from angry and slightly terrifying middle-class women. I had been sin-binned for a score of years as a result of this. My *New Collected Poems* (Kardoorair Press, 2012) was virtually ignored by the literati – after sixty years of application to the craft of verse! Welcome to Literature!

Erwin Zehentner: It's a tricky one. If you get too feral, you are dismissed as a radical and get sued. Alternativeely, if you support the current leadership, you are seen as a sycophant. And what happens if the leadership changes? Can't win. My thought is to (generally) make sly digs at politicians reflecting some of the past things said and pointing out the error of said utterances.

Do you think poetry's primary function has changed through recent emphasis on performance in the visual age?

Phi Radmall: No, I don't think so. There will always be different elements of writing and performing and always have been. The word is the thing.

Candy Royalle: I believe there are those who will seek out poetry in the medium that best suits them. I think that people are drawn to performance poetry events because of that need to connect with community. I believe people feel very disconnected and performance poetry enables people to connect with each other, listen to beautiful work and share that experience with others.

Willem Tibben: No, I think just the delivery system for the poetry weapon has changed. I'm with Wallace Stevens as quoted by Michael Sharkey recently: '…poetry "must give pleasure". Pleasure is not the same thing as fun. Poetry can supply something more enduring, an entry into deeper thought and emotions and be, as John Keats said, "a friend".'

Martin Langford: I don't think its primary function has ever changed – to explore the human condition in words – and, if you're good enough, to make that sing. Performance poetry can be more conservative than page poetry, confirming what the audience already thinks. Much too little performance poetry takes real risks with meanings. Page poetry tends to have more opportunities to be exploratory – but these descriptions are ignored often enough, and the two forms are joined at the hip.

Edwin Wilson: Poetry is very much an archaic art form, from preliterate societies when wandering bards helped share the tribal legends – with rhyme being used as a mnemonic or an aid to memory. The development of the printing press made poetry almost obsolete, with the wandering bard being replaced by rock 'n' roll, and the touring bands of roadies in our highly visual age. The Beatles were the band of my youth, and true poets – while their early lyrics were not so hot, the lyrics of some of the songs that preceded them, like 'Mashed Potatoes Yeah!' were pure and unadulterated pap. The Beatles spoke to me of my world as I was experiencing it – some of their draft lyrics in a glass case in the British Museum were treated like religious relics. Bob Dylan was/is a true poet and took his name from Dylan Thomas.

Cathy Bray: I believe poets are still trying to deliver their understanding of the truth or the reality as they perceive it. I believe that some performance poets can actually divert the audience's attention from the poetry.

Kate Lilley: I don't think it's changed.

Benito di Fonzo: Art is something useless and beautiful that makes us feel human. Always was, always will be…

Les Wicks: I'm not sure the balance has changed that much. Back in the 1970s a lot of the performance poetry was starting to morph into stand-up comedy and of course the street forms were in their early infancy.

David Falcon: Poetry like all good art can be different things to different people at different times. There is a place for intimate conversation and a place for a public address. It is the versatility of the poetic form that allows it to function in so many ways. There may be times when the consuming public turns more to one medium than another but that does not change the function of poetry. On the face of it, you might say that poetry in one setting is functioning as light entertainment and at others as a doorway to introspection, but nevertheless, if it deserves the name, poetry will speak powerfully to us about our humanity and in that, its function, it does not change.

Paul Buckberry: Two things about poetry and the digital age, one good the other bad. The good thing about the digital age and poetry is that anyone can publish a poem. The bad thing about the digital age and poetry is that anyone can publish a poem.

Scott Sandwich: If anything, poetry is going back to its roots in oral histories, isn't it? Come to think of it, I'm not even sure what the primary function of poetry is, because the functions of poetry, surely, range from entertainment and expression and questions and answers and stories and sound and blah blah blah… Those things can't change, and sometimes those functions aren't even there and…hang on, what is poetry? Is this poetry? But it doesn't even rhyme!

Richard James Allen: I have worked with poetry and dance, film, theatre, music, radio, new media and so on. But I have also just written a book of poetry, *Fixing the Broken Nightingale*, the aim of which is completely to reiterate the traditional values and functions of poetry, which I also adore.

How do you/would you get a person interested in poetry?

Edwin Wilson: The pathways to poetry for young people today may be through the best music in the popular culture. When my son John was about thirteen, I saw some lyrics written in his hand on a piece of paper left on his bed, and thought I had sired a genius. The words were the lyrics to some current song but they were very good. In my day, I was influenced by inspired teachers – by my old primary school headmaster, Bill Bouveret; by my high school English teacher, Walt Wardman; and by Paul Lamb, my poetry lecturer at Armidale Teachers' College, who first exposed me to A.E. Housman – at the age of seventeen. And I was hooked.

Erwin Zehentner: Don't know that one. My interest was triggered when Robert Balas showed me his first book of poetry, *Once Upon a Place, Twice Upon a Moon*, which combined art with words. The rich, romantic imagery prompted me to start a series of artworks – I did about twelve Moons in a series – two of which found favour with a paying customer.

Paul Buckberry: Music is often a good place to start. Drawing focus to a musical performer's lyrics. Knowing the person you are trying to interest is an advantage. It's easier to find a poet who may inspire if the person you are trying to inspire is a friend.

Phil Radmall: Read a good poem to them.

Les Wicks: There is no one answer and that is the only question!

Kate Lilley: Share my own passionate interest in it.

Candy Royalle: I take them to a performance poetry event and give them a copy of one of my favourite poet's books.

Willem Tibben: Maybe by chatting about it…especially striking the person with a poem that seems to be speaking about what that person is moved/grabbed by/interested in – I can't bring an example to mind…leave this one with me.

Susan Adams: Poets have to know words and have some language understanding – it can be purely spoken/vocalised energy and emotion but it must resonate with them.

Cathy Bray: Attraction rather than promotion – by introducing them first to the poets of their own culture and place so that can readily recognise themselves or their own landscape – physical and emotional – in the poetry.

Benito di Fonzo: Gaffer tape, drugs and an occy strap… Or better still, make it fun, exciting and accessible, like the Beat poets did – that's what got me into it.

Richard James Allen: Poetry is the language of the soul, our deepest inner voice. Ask someone to listen to a poem imagining that they are hearing, perhaps clearly for the first time, intuitions previously barely acknowledged, as they lie in bed, unable to sleep, late into the night. My poetry isn't just about me voicing my own thoughts, it's reminding people to listen to their own.

Scott Sandwich: People are interested in poetry. If someone says they don't like poetry, that's as close-minded as saying, 'I don't like songs.' Poetry is such a huge umbrella term, it's not always complex, or funny, or abstract, or ridiculous, or political, or earnest, or funny… Poetry doesn't have to be anything. I've met many people who say they don't like poetry because they think it's a very specific type of art, or always in the same form, not something broad. It's just about helping others understand that poetry isn't just one thing, just like all songs don't have to sound like the Beatles in 1962. Failing that, a dirty limerick never goes astray.

Martin Langford: They must be exposed to satisfying experiences with poetry: that's the basis for engagement with any art. It does seem to be a brutal art form – I think it's harder to offer satisfying experiences than it sounds, and I suspect many punters turn away after brief explorations because they don't find what they're looking for. And then you have to make sure you can offer them subsequent quality experiences on a predictable basis! It would also help if poets – or at least the poetry – were treated with a bit more respect. There is a subtle ambivalence about the respect poetry is given in Australian public spaces. This isn't helped by the behaviour of the poets. Poets should treat their own work with respect, and MCs should honour that. Neither of those things always happens. That said, Don Bank has done and continues to do a terrific job: congratulations on the twenty-five years!

2015

February 25th. There were two guys from out of town to open the batting for the year. Brendan Doyle from the Blue Mountains said the title of his book *Glass Bicycles* referred to his poems – fragile but hopefully able to find a passage over any terrain. Brendan ran the gamut of subjects from the naivety of 'Newtown Boy' (his first big hit) to 'Shells' and 'Iraqi Moon Over Mosman', which made telling social points.

Ben Hession from Wollongong has a reputation for conjuring a modern mini-series around characters in Greek mythology. He didn't disappoint this night. He's also not beyond making adroit comments on contemporary life and times. He reflected in his interview on his times as a rock MC on community radio keeping him abreast of what youth is on about.

Among the open section readers, Garry McDougall took us on a journey to Pezenas in Southern France in the footsteps of Molière. The convenor recalled meeting the ghost of Grace Perry as he was cleaning out the study and then spent evenings besotted by her work, which treated poetry like some 'unwelcome but inescapable intimate in the body'. This was linked to unhappy consequences Grace suffered at the hands of the poetry establishment in the 1970s before her suicide at her Berrima farm.

Kerry Jamieson reported back on the quixotic treatment of Emily Dickinson's work in a book she won at Don Bank last November. Jennifer Nixon was on fire with a timely revisit to 'Razorwire' from *Open Boat – Barbed Wire Sky: Poems by and for Refugees* and a new poem, 'Frontier Land'.

A feature of the night that proved very popular was American satirist David Bader's haikus on the great works of literature which peppered the convenor's adlib between poems. To quote one example, *Waiting for Godot* by Samuel Beckett. 'Act one.

It's hopeless. My boots don't fit. Where is God? Act Two. The same thing.'

This was one of the warmest February readings in atmosphere at the Bank for some years. I was suddenly gladdened to overhear this comment during supper: 'I've probably picked up more about poetry and how it works in so many life situations at places like Live Poets than anywhere else.'

March 25th. Two very distinct forms of listening ensued at this meeting with the headline acts – Judith Beveridge and David Stavanger. To Judith's soft tones the audience leaned close to absorb the intricacies of story. Stavanger by contrast set the crowd back on its heels with his more confrontational presentation. Judith is one of our most respected poets, with five landmark books, teaching poetry at Uni of Sydney and being poetry editor at *Meanjin*, as well as tirelessly launching other people's projects. This was a welcome return for her to Don Bank. She broke new ground with her *Domesticity of Giraffes* in 1987, which won several major awards and contained poems which ended up in the Australian school curriculum. She had written about spiritual figures before, and the story of Devadatta – with his joining Siddhartha's group to work against it from within, his coveting of Siddhartha's wife, his attempts to kill the Buddha – has material suitable for a pot-boiler. But Judith wanted to write 'Devadatta's Poems' in such a way that a truth can be gleaned without resorting to a beginning, a middle and an end. Even more telling than his thwarted ambitions was Devadatta's mindset when he is finally resigned to living the lowliest existence among the detritus on the jungle floor.

David Stavanger runs poetry slams and is a director of the Quennsland Poetry Festival and his books are published by UQP. This night he was less concerned with explaining he was a lapsed psychiatrist and bipolar than tickling the audience's reactions with a head doctor's tricks. His poetry was delivered bluffly, almost grudgingly, but there was a calculating effect there too.

In the first half, Justin Sheining from North Sydney Council was on hand to tell us about events to mark the council's 125th anniversary in July and hear of Live Poets' plans to welcome Sydney's poets of the 1890s to Don Bank cottage and farm. This convenor also performed a poem to camera – part of an occasional series to feature work from overseas. Tonight it was 'The Clock' by La Shawna Tallisha of Barbados.

Two features of the open section: Bill Tibben's reflections on the hundred years of Anzac exhibition, Then, Now, Tomorrow – After the War, at Peacock Gallery, Auburn, centring on our unappreciated Aboriginal soldiers. And Eileen Chong's first visit to Don Bank after many moons of hearing about it. Her poem 'Circle' about the death then the wedding of a friend whetted our appetite for more. Wonder of wonders we were done by 10.15 p.m. to the strains of Salif Keita on the beatbox.

A Peaceful Time

hot oil on a medium gold flame
gently place in it a cluster of black mustard seeds

hear the crackle, let the journey begin
white diced new potatoes go in next
white salt, red pepper, yellow turmeric
sprinkle, a teaspoon of each

a little white sugar   all mixed together

just enough colourless water for the potatoes to cook

cover the pan

let your mind rest for a while
those thoughts, let them pass over your head
my mind door is closed at present, you say
I am cooking a Gujarati potato curry

are the potatoes cooked? Yes, if a fork
pierces through the potatoes

sprinkle some yellowy orangey coriander powder

garnish with some deep green coriander leaves
squeeze a few drops of yellow lemon juice

look at the sky, breathe in
and slowly eat the flavours, colours with rice & bread
is your heart satisfied?
adjust as necessary.

Bhupen Thakker

Glass Mirror

Don't stare at me like this!
Do you hear me? Stop it!
Do you have to mimic me?
Do you? Answer me!
You consume all that's around you
how hungry can you be?
You attract everyone with your gaze
are you so pretty?
You force yourself into the smallest gap
you are so intrusive!
Are you telling me the truth?
Don't you like to lie?
You are so satiated
but are you?
It took one careless move
for your glass tears to flow
leaving behind a minute emptiness
within an enormous space.

Olga Kulanowska

Scenes from a Twenty-four-hour News Channel

(A desultory sonnet)

– Hypocrite lecteur, – mon semblable, – mon frère!

Sorry, excuse me, I need to put down my glass.
Ah, there's Mary. I should go and say hello, and there's…
The music here is just so loud. And do I smell grass?
Mary's excitedly talking to Paul: who, stoned, stares.

Who's that dj mixing? The West? No, it's really okay.
Hi Mary (hugs). Hi Paul. Yes? Do I what? Pardon?
Well, I still do the radio. I try to write every day.
You've read somewhere? Can I get a jealous hard-on?

I can't hear a thing. It's too hot. Sorry. I think I need
some air. Pooh. Who farted? Look, Paul's disappeared.
Mary, yes, dance the vibrator. I can smell more weed.
Am I shocked by this place? No, it's just sort of weird.

I'm tired. I'm going. Yeah. Good night. Catching the train.
Home fast. Now, what's on TV? Bombing in Syria again.

Ben Hession

River Music

The mouth of a little fish had just sipped away a star
from the river, a lyrebird was opening the day, volunteering
to be a bell. We were watching an egret prod at the nutrient
dark, its beak one tine of a fork catching what floats, just
as the sun began cracking the trees awake. The bird's song

reached us, then it sharded into the river's cold glass.
You thought you heard it again in the eddying backwash.
A frog began to ratchet, self-correcting like a clock. Our
boat swung away on the revolutions of its propeller, water
adjusted its slap, displacing sound in the cutaway rock

and then the egret stepped into a sun-shaft; a crow flew
down, made its slain-in-the-spirit human sound. Cicadas
drummed hard against a sky turning cold, vitrified. Wind
came, then the rain. Then the wind dropped into the reeds
though you said it was the bird again and its sly alarm.

We found hooks enough to load our lines, let our reels
click the hours away with the quick flicking of our casts.
I heard a bird fly into the pin oaks, the swamp gums, then
into the tupelos with barely a sound. All the way home
I turned the oars hard, making a round music with my arms.

Judith Beveridge

The Clock

Sometimes I admire a clock.
It may seem strange, weird, dumb –
but yes I do!
Cause I wish I could have the attributes that a clock has *fah trute*!
A clock holds time captive,
inside his face,
with its hands squeezing the digits on the passcode,
to open the time vault.
Hmm – the clock is something that I admire.
As I watch it simply sitting on its throne,
and making persons fret, quarrel, cuss about how the time has flown.
Come on! This clock is a serious outlaw!
Too bad many of you did not know
that the clock is the king of malice,
as it can manipulate its hands to speed up time,
creating panic and uneasiness…
Imagine if I had that attribute.
Wouldn't the world be a better place?
Maybe?
Maybe not?
But still the clock,
when properly trained,
can be an accurate source of time,
and help persons to relax and unwind,
and enjoy the company of friends.
That is, until the clock is ready to share malice again and its two arms reach the twelve,
and all the time is gone.
It smiles and looks at the world shouting:
'Let the Games Begin!'

La Shawna Talisha

Night Graffiti

I don't write love poems any more.
'Love doesn't last' you said.
So, is this greenhouse heat
that fogs your window glass
with blinds drawn fast –
and logic checked in artificial light?

I've seen twin leaves pressed for time –
throughout a winter's night
swelling out – with signatures of spring
beneath the covers –
that fine print leaves its mark
on interlocking lovers.

I've known the freeze-dried feel
of times apart:
numbed in keen winds
of this raw city.
Drawn to its heart. I've watched your name
scrawled high on rough red walls.

I don't write love poems any more
'It doesn't last' you said.
Yet cordite sparks my veins as I ignite
enveloped here behind this polished glass
these flames, cast in the night,
light up your name.

Jill Carter-Hansen

Reunion of the Source

This is a reunion of the source all the way from the beginning of being.

How should we foster efforts to talk
while already starting to walk together?

All the travel that happens throughout the summer
breaking out from the ring of forgotten games of mutual puzzle.

For the ultimate truth of jigsaw puzzles
is the fading trace of every piece we moved.

We are both now in an uncommon room instead of love.

Nobody searched for us.

It's a year paid for by the careful attention
and the rippling reflections that we have shared
during this series of disappearances of life.

We should foster efforts to keep plowing on with
the invisible chances hovering overhead.

You are a few infinite hours more than a whole life.
My time is to go outside for a while to imprint
these clearer moments that sometimes silently
called and invited us to stay inside each other,
sheltered in the architecture of our conversation.

We're letting go soon, we two whirling avian dervishes,
and absence is growing on us.

Why do we have to solve our mystery?

Today is a sensitive language exchanged
by the pulse of our touching hands.

Give thanks for all yours. All yours. All your. All you.

Hamish Danks Brown

Bathurst Street

I always said that I lived on Bathurst Street
My gateway into the city
Disembarking from the bus line
On the corner of Elizabeth Street

Always running late to work tripping up my well-heeled step
Navigating my way down Bathurst Street

Once seeing the ambulance light flash on the corner of
George Street
A motorcyclist down critical
A pedestrian lay dead on Bathurst Street

Now I darken on Bathurst Street
Je sombré dans Bathurst Street
Now I die on Bathurst Street

Je sombre sur Bathurst Street
Je crève sur Bathurst Street
Maintenant je suis morte sur Bathurst Street

The crime scene of where we first met

You walking towards me lost after midnight
In front of the Edinburgh Castle Hotel
On the corner of Pitt Street

I had innocent intentions then
To enlighten you of the Western ways here
From your petroleum wealth nation there

And tonight white rain falls
That other white flashes neon sparks across the sky
Sounds of red and blue flashing lights fill the air

I wish they were here to collect me
Enclosed within another four walls
However with no key in my dress pocket

Then I think of your delicate young pink lips blossoming
The arch of your aquiline nose
Those clichéd large almond-shaped eyes

The ethno cyber funk plays on the radio
A shout out to you
Our names sing out in harmony
Pronounced together on the airwaves
A little radio frequency prayer from me

Abdul Salam & Fayroze

I promised myself I would never let you touch me

I am ten years your senior

The last time we met late night at the sandstone station exit
On the corner of Elizabeth and Foveaux Streets
You then told me you were to leave
Exiled three years
Your papers not in order
I took you to the nearest body of water
Darling Harbour
As we sat I began to cry
Cursing this city of mine

As we walked you told me it was your birthday
And for a woman that never sings I sang Happy Birthday
For you to you
Out loud on Pyrmont Bridge
Shouting, 'Hip hip hooray'
On that old bridge

I finally gave in to you that night
Our bodies mixed
Twisted and knotted together

Your very taste…
Your white blood could heal sins

Ten years my junior

And the police sirens don't stop at my door

The other night whilst on George Street
Confusion, longing filled every cubic centimetre of me
I ran towards where we first met

Thinking if I could just get back to Bathurst Street
That I would somehow find you on Bathurst Street
That my breath would ease on Bathurst Street

Knowing that I once lived on Bathurst Street

Fayroze Lutta

To the whales at Warrnambool

(after Thomas Moore)

It is said
about the dark night of the soul
that when you're in the belly of the whale
and all that you are experiencing
is blackness and stillness
and nobody knows where you are
least of all yourself
and it feels like every day there is
no change
and nothing

that the thing to know
is that the whale is always moving

your job
is simply this:

to be ready
when the time comes

and the whale
spits you out.

onto a new shore.

Beth Spencer

My Teacher Fish

You must be screwed up man
A teacher? HELL
A teacher TEACHES.
He don't know the outdoor stuff.
He don't care.
He'd never walk by himself
Before breakfast
Across fields
Getting his feet soaked
Just to fish.
He teaches.

He marks papers
Or he reads books
He don't fish with no 2-ounce rod
And lay that long line easy on the top
Like this here… LOOK
Oh, man.
Don't tell me he hears them wild birds
He don't
He don't know the inside feel
Or white water rushin'
Cold against his knees
He don't know fishin', man.
Not like me.

Jim Quealey

Stormy Ocean

Endless ocean stormy sea
Take us to a land that's free
A land of sunshine way down south
We've heard ALL about by word of mouth

It's a land so vast a land so bold
Where no one's EVER left out in the cold
Where the people are friendly the people are kind
You're a penniless outcast they don't mind

They welcome you with a big hello
They offer you food take you to see a show
They know where you come from is living hell
They beat you they starve you they throw you in jail

They know 'bout the smuggler he take thousands of bucks
HE don't care you're down on your luck
HE don't care if the boat roll over
We all perish HE's in clover

Sure hope we make it to that promised land
Where the people they take you by the hand
THEY don't care you're brown yellow black

There's no way in the world they'd send you back
STORMY OCEAN take me there
Land of my dreams Australia Fair.

Amory Hill

Circle

'ankles as tiny and spare as a bird's' – Jason Dunne, 'Everyone is Henry Miller'

In the churchyard the people have gathered,
sombre as crows. You're in a dark suit,
your eyes emptied, shadowed. Around you,
friends and family, rumpled and in shock –

everyone ants scurrying around the great roots
of the fig trees, two hundred year old Moreton Bays,
sending electrical signals of loss and dismay
along scent trails. The bamboo groves

have outgrown imagination, they belong
on some movie set with acrobats –
your sparrow laid out in her coffin,
lowered into sacred ground. You wed

in that church. She must have worn heels beneath
her dress – stilettos, perhaps – but underneath the lengths
no one could tell as she glided down the aisle towards you
and the both of you, young and in love, said 'I do. I do. I do.'

Eileen Chong

Basra

he picks up his fishing net
takes two buckets
leaves the third one at home
she packs him two loaves of bread
a cucumber, half a tomato and some milk
in a glass bottle
he kisses her forehead
walks to the river
rolls up his pants above the knee
(the water is softer than summer)
it whispers through his toes
he slices the river with his net
the birds chirp
the lazy ones stared
(Sam Cooke on the soundtrack)
he would've been 85 today.

Ahmad Al Rady

Towards Melaleuca

First warning –
the euphoria of perspective loss.
I'm flying with Kerry Bird
who's made over a thousand journeys
into this deceitful blue.
But landlubbers like the endangered yellow-bellied parrot,
like myself,
should never get this high.

Second warning:
that shuddering eddy – not dropping – dropping!
The hands guiding you through the gusty ether – get careless!
I looked down instinctively:
you'd be rejected there, too
where the springy-couch of button-grass
is only productive after fire;
never to be built upon by man.

We bank to avoid an updraught:
'Always leave a back-door escape route open'
said the Bird
as, through chasing thunderheads,
the cotton-wool epicentre was opening;
describing a perfect, icy blossom.

My mind, aghast at the spiral, stabbed for the words

'Third warning…'

Danny Gardner

Afterword – 22 April 2015

The clouds were black overhead when we got to the venue and we knew there were challenges ahead. As the rain began to come down while we were bringing the chairs in from the store shed, we knew it would be a severe test of loyalty for anyone to turn up that night of the venue's twenty-fifth anniversary – even those not inconvenienced by the calamitous weather over the last three days. Yet we had to bring celebratory decorations, food and drink to cater for a big group regardless. We'd done all the prep with forty-five minutes to spare. Helen had said, 'Let's be realistic – don't put all the chairs out.'

I put on a CD of English roots music and had just started to set up the front table when Diane was knocking at the side door. Then Jamal and Mohsen arrived and, shortly after, Martin Ellis, North Sydney Council's Leisure Director. It appears his appointment at HMAS *Penguin* had been an early one. We had a good chat about some of the characters Live Poets had hosted over the last decade, many of them pictured on one of our poster boards dressing the sitting room. This took my mind off worrying how many more people would turn up – or not.

But suddenly there were more voices at the door, then an SMS on my phone from Bee, who I hadn't expected to show, coming up from the Gong. The SMS said, 'sorry'. There was another SMS but I was then greeted by Geoff, last seen in the 1990s, who had seen the article in the local paper and had rung me at home. I recognised him now but he had not brought his keyboard. That knocked out any live music on the night probably – a bad loss. But I was soon greeting more people – Helen Wren; Doug Nicholls, a blast from the more recent past; Moree Ward, who had featured in our 2001 anthology. And now here were Bee and Allan coming around the corner after all, after having all but turned back in the worsening conditions en route – just before they sent that first SMS –- but who had decided to battle on and were delighted to get to North Sydney and have no parking problems. And they were raring to go with music to start the show!

'Fallen on your feet again, Danny,' Martin commented.

Acknowledgements

Susan Adams, The Donation, *Southerly 2012* & *International Language and Literature Forum, (China) 2012* & *Australian Poetry Anthology (Au) 2013*
Robert Adamson, Carnaby's Cockatoo, *Net Needle*
Ludwika Amber, Australian Language Landscape, *Our Territory*
Robert Balas, So you took a trip, *Open Twenty Four Hours*
Emily Ballou, Marriage, *The Darwin Poems*
Judith Beveridge, River Music, *Storm and Honey*
Margaret Bradstock, Mingmarriya Country, *Barnacle Rock*
Michelle Cahill, Parvati in Darlinghurst, *Vishvarupa*
Cherie, Dumpling, *Moonlight of Romance*
Christina Conrads, Round flat tin, *Illusion's Hump*
Peter Doyle, Of Poetry, *The Museum of Space*
Dexter Dunphy, Carapace, *Strange Wings*
Dan Eggs, The Fridge is Pregnant, CD *Rhythmical Psalms of the Skiing Continuum*, Vol .1
Danny Gardner, Towards Melaleuca, *Before I Press the Trigger*
Clark Gormley, A Spade by any other name, *Turn of Phrase*
Keith Hansen, Eveleigh Street, *Hollow Moon and Terrace Houses*
Ross Hattaway, The New Cooking, *Pretending to be Dead*
Elisabeth Hodgson, Sometimes the man and his wife go away, *skin painting*
Jackson, the moon on her setting arc, Winner Ethel Webb Bundell Literary Awards 2014
Fadeel Kayat, Public Tree, *Auburn Letters*
Bogdan Koca, The Poem That Escaped, *Mood Lightning Poetry Anthology*
Martin Langford, At the Olympics: Handball, *Meanjin*
Kate Lilley, Almanac, *Ladylike*
Charles Lovecraft, Red Sails, *Ramblings from an Attic Mind*
Roberta Lowing, By Ourselves, Nothing?, *Ruin*
Dorothy Makasa, *Ubuntu e chalo* – Our humanity a Universe, *Auburn Letters*

Dennis McDermott, The Up Train, *Dorothy's Skin*
Anna Kerdijk Nicholson, The Dig Tree, *The Disappearing* (The Red Room Company project), *Everyday Epic*
Louise Oxley, Listening for the road, *Australian Poetry Journal 11*
Phyllis Perlstone, Their eyes disturb us, *The Edge of Everything*
Sheryl Persson, Transported, *Building Dreams, DiVerse*
Craig Powell, Happy Endings, *Music and Women's Bodies*
Brian Purcell, Tunnel of Ants, *Ten Years Live*
David Reiter, Dancing Sinatra, *My Planets*
Brenda Saunders, Sonnet, *156th Sonnet Anthology*,
Henry Sheerwater, Sunday Sailor, *Bare Ground, Bare Feet: poetry serving Gaia*
Steve Smart, NYC – poetry bars, *Jars of Memory*
Beth Spencer, To the whales at Warrnambool, *Vagabondage*
Randall Stephens, Sorry, *One For the Road*
Billy Marshall Stoneking, I Have Poems, *Maya and the Real Stuff*
William Tibben, My Shoe Box ID, *the fascination of what's simple*
Tineke Van der Eecken, For Séraphine, *Language*
Christopher Wallace-Crabbe, Garlic, *Domestic Subline*
David Wansbrough, The Ordinary Order of Things, *Mood Lightning*
Kyla Lee Ward, Herbal Tea, *The Land of Bad Dreams*
Maurice Whelan, Small Beginnings, *The Lilac Bow*
Cecilia White, Boxing Day Test, Winner 2011 International Cricket Poetry prize
Ketut Yuliarsa, Stranded Noah's Ark, *Jatuh Bisu – Falling in Silence*
Dona Samson Zappone, Letter from OZ, *Colours of Life* (UK)

*

The yearly reviews are personal recollections of the convenor. The answers to questions in Poetry and Presenting it to the Public have been edited for space reasons.

Thanks

North Sydney Council for their generous, unstinting support for our time at Don Bank cottage.

Helen Lu for her hot suppers (always!) but particularly in the winter months.

Bill (Willem) Tibben for his perennial help in running the show.

George Clarke for his special liquid refreshment.

The media – particularly Kate Crawford and the *Mosman Daily* – who've done so many stories on us.

Special mentions to Ken Bock at 2RPH and David and Robyn at MiSociety.

Blues Point Bookshop, Antique Bookshop and Crows Nest Half-Back Exchange, Pages and Pages, Mosman – and the Stanton, Mosman and Manly Libraries – who display our monthly notices.

Those poets and musicians (unofficially but no less affectionately known as the Live Poets Players) who've helped us mount our various special performances.

Those people who help put the chairs back in the shed at the end of the night.

All the poets and musicians who have read or played at Live Poets @ Don Bank and all those people who've come to listen and 'discuss over supper in the courtyard' over so many years. You are the reason we open the door.

www.ingramcontent.com/pod-product-compliance
Lightning Source LLC
Chambersburg PA
CBHW071803080526
44589CB00012B/660